ENCOUNTER
WITH
THE
HOLY
SPIRIT

ENCOUNTER
WITH
THE
HOLY
SPIRIT

Geo. R. Brunk II, Editor

HERALD PRESS
SCOTTDALE, PENNSYLVANIA
1972

ENCOUNTER WITH THE HOLY SPIRIT

Copyright © 1972 by Herald Press, Scottdale, Pa. 15683
Library of Congress Catalog Card Number: 72-2053
International Standard Book Number: 0-8361-1693-3

Printed in United States

FOREWORD

One of the impressive developments of our time has to do with the new interest in the person and work of the Holy Spirit.

A tidal wave of enthusiasm appears to be moving across the various denominations with reference to the gifts and manifestations of the Spirit.

Many Christians agree that with few exceptions the doctrine of the Holy Spirit has been neglected by the denominations generally. We are now witnessing what is being called the Charismatic Renewal Movement. The term "charismatic" is used frequently in connection with the practice of speaking in tongues. Actually, the charismatic term applies to the total theology of the Holy Spirit in His anointing presence and power in the life of the believer.

The charismatic movement, if properly understood, is most certainly one of the favorable developments of our time. This new focus of attention on the doctrine of the Holy Spirit seems to be long overdue and may be one of the answers to the needs of the contemporary church. Is it possible that our lack of success in the work of evangelism may be attributable in part to our neglect of this great doctrine? It appears from the book of Acts and the entire New Testament that the doctrine of the Holy Spirit had a very large place in the life of the church.

It is recognized of course that there is considerable difference of opinion among Christians with reference to the person and work of the Holy Spirit. The glossolalia aspect has perhaps been the point at which there has been sharpest difference of opinion, but other areas also have lacked clarity and unanimity within the Christian fellowship.

It is a pleasure to bring together the papers that were presented at the Consultation on the Person and Work of the Holy Spirit at Eastern Mennonite College, January 18-21, 1972. The interest in this Consultation ran far beyond expectations. Rarely has there been any event on EMC campus of such a nature drawing people from so many circles far and near.

The reader will discover that there were differences of interpretation and that various points of view were presented. Interesting conversation followed each presentation. Despite the differences, there was a spirit of genuine Christian brotherhood in which all participants were free to express themselves. There was general agreement that the Spirit of God was present, as we moved together in a sincere effort to understand what the Scripture has to say on this important doctrine.

There was strong interest on the part of participants in having these papers made available for careful study. It is with the hope that the church will be blessed and that the Lord of the church will be exalted that this symposium is published.

> Geo. R. Brunk II, Dean
> Eastern Mennonite Seminary
> Harrisonburg, Va.

March 27, 1972

CONTENTS

1

THE
HOLY SPIRIT
IN EXALTATION
OF
CHRIST

By Geo. R. Brunk II

While we as participants may measure the success of this Consultation subjectively, that is by what it has done to us or by how it has made us feel, God is appraising it by an entirely different standard. The focal question therefore would seem to be, not, How have I been made to feel? but rather, How well has Jesus Christ been exalted in our conversation here concerning the Holy Spirit? In fact, we may say that this is the real question with reference to the total life and witness of the Christian.

The above conclusion is based upon two passages of Scripture in particular. We note first the words of our Lord as recorded in John 15:26, 27:

But when the Comforter is come, whom I will send unto you from the Father, even the Spirit of truth, which proceedeth from the Father, he shall testify of me:

And ye also shall bear witness because ye have been with me from the beginning.

The word order of the same passage in the Greek original is interesting, significant, and emphatic.

When comes the Comforter whom I will send to you from the Father, the Spirit of the truth which from the Father proceeds, that one will witness concerning me; also ye and witness, because from (the) beginning with me ye are.

Observe the two occurrences of the word "witness." The Holy Spirit will witness concerning Christ. We also will witness concerning Him.

The second passage referred to above is found in John 16:13 and 14. Let us again notice the King James reading and then the order of these words in the Greek text.

Howbeit when he, the Spirit of truth, is come, he will guide you into all truth: for he shall not speak of himself; but whatsoever he shall hear, that shall he speak: and he will shew you things to come.

He shall glorify me: for he shall receive of mine, and shall shew it unto you.

Notice now where the emphasis rests according to the word order and sequence in the original:

But when comes that one, the Spirit of truth, he will guide you into the truth all; for not will he speak from himself, but what things he hears he will speak, and the coming things he will announce to you.

That one me will glorify, because of the of me he will receive and will announce to you.

In these two passages we have very much needed but often neglected aspects of the theology of the Holy Spirit. Without due attention to these aspects we would be remiss in our 2 1/2 days of study and conversation concerning the third person of the Godhead. Perhaps it has been assumed by all that we would come to grips with the truth here presented in John 15 and 16 before the Consultation ended.

Let us now proceed to notice specifically what it is that our Lord teaches us in the above passages concerning the Holy Spirit who is referred to in chapter 16 as the Spirit of truth and in chapter 15 as the Comforter.

It should be noted that the Holy Spirit is the Comforter of whom Jesus said, "I will send unto you from the Father even the Spirit of truth which proceedeth from the Father." We need not here enter into the age-old debate of the church fathers as to whether the Spirit "proceedeth" from both the Father and the Son or not. It is clear that He the Spirit would be sent by the Son and that He would proceed from the Father. This may raise questions about the Christian doctrine of the Trinity, which lies beyond our comprehension, but which is nevertheless assumed and accepted in the Scripture even though the word "Trinity" does not occur in the Bible. The doctrine of the Trinity is not to be thought of as a matter of little importance in the issue before us concerning the Spirit's work in the exaltation of Christ.

So much for the "coming" of the Spirit. What about His "doing"?

"He will guide you into all truth." Are we able to comprehend this great statement? Not truth only. How wonderful to have truth without the admixture of error. But He will guide into all truth. This includes the truth about the Spirit which we together have sought with such openness these days. But in the light of the full statement it must have primary reference to the truth concerning the Son. Let us thank God for the truth and for our access to all of the truth that really matters!

On the negative side we learn here that the Spirit will not speak of (or from) Himself. He will speak what He hears and will show things to come. In other words it is not His task to focus attention upon Himself. He is not an end in Himself but rather a divine means to an end, the exaltation of Jesus Christ.

This then brings us to the climactic point of both passages:

"He [the Spirit] shall testify of me."

"He [the Spirit] shall glorify me."

The focal point of the total ministry of the Holy Spirit is therefore the exaltation of Christ! He will not speak of Himself. He will glorify Christ. This reminds us of Jesus who sought not His own glory but the glory of the Father who sent Him. Jesus also said that His teaching was not His own but "His that sent me."

There remains a very practical point in all of this. What are the implications for us as disciples of Christ?

10

We have seen that the Spirit would witness concerning Christ. But the disciples also are to witness concerning Him as stated in John 15:27. Does this not include us? Most certainly it does.

Even when we experience some striking visitation of the Spirit in our own lives, we will leave no listener under the impression that we exalt any other person than Jesus Christ. Surely not ourselves nor any other human instrument who may have been used of God as a channel of blessing. Our "boast" must, as with the Apostle Paul, be in God. A testimony of blessing in the Spirit that fails to exalt Christ fails the test of Scripture.

If we can in some sense comprehend the centrality of Christ in all the sweep of history, particularly in the eternity to come, perhaps we can better understand the importance of exalting Him by the Spirit through the church in this present time.

John says, "In the beginning was the Word, and the Word was with God, and the Word was God. . . . All things were made by him; and without him was not any thing made that was made." We all of course understand that Jesus Christ was from eternity and that we have appearances of the Lord Jesus Christ in the Old Testament.

We think of Jesus Christ in the incarnation as the incarnate Christ, God in the flesh. This of course staggers our imagination and lies beyond our comprehension, but it is true. We have the record of His birth, His life, His suffering, His death, His resurrection from the dead, and His ascension into heaven. There we see the glory of the incarnate One.

In Scripture we see the Christ of the eternity to

come. The Christ of the future is revealed to us in the Book of Revelation.

The following passages express something of the highest tributes paid to Him in heaven:

Revelation 5:11-14:

And I beheld, and I heard the voice of many angels round about the throne and the beasts and the elders: and the number of them was ten thousand times ten thousand, and thousands of thousands;

Saying with a loud voice, Worthy is the Lamb that was slain to receive power, and riches, and wisdom, and strength, and honour, and glory, and blessing.

And every creature which is in heaven, and on the earth, and under the earth, and such as are in the sea, and all that are in them, heard I saying, Blessing, and honour, and glory, and power, be unto him that sitteth upon the throne, and unto the Lamb for ever and ever.

And the four beasts said, Amen. And the four and twenty elders fell down and worshipped him that liveth for ever and ever.

Revelation 7:11-17:

And all the angels stood round about the throne, and about the elders and the four beasts, and fell before the throne on their faces, and worshipped God,

Saying, Amen: Blessing, and glory, and wisdom, and thanksgiving, and honour, and power, and might, be unto our God for ever and ever. Amen.

And one of the elders answered, saying unto me, What are these which are arrayed in white robes? and whence came they?

And I said unto him, Sir, thou knowest. And he said to me, These are they which came out of great tribulation, and have washed their robes, and made them white in the blood of the Lamb.

Therefore are they before the throne of God, and serve him day and night in his temple: and he that sitteth on the throne shall dwell among them.

They shall hunger no more, neither thirst any more; neither shall the sun light on them, nor any heat.

For the Lamb which is in the midst of the throne shall feed them, and shall lead them unto living fountains of waters: and God shall wipe away all tears from their eyes.

It is clear then, that Christ's position is one of great glory both in the eternity of the past and in the eternity of the future. But the whole point of this presentation has to do with the Christ of the present and the glory which is to be ascribed to Him presumably here on earth throughout the church age. Let us remember the words of Jesus when He said the Holy Spirit would witness concerning Him and we too would do the same. Perhaps it is by means of and through the Christians that the Holy Spirit would witness of, speak of, and glorify Christ. In some sense certainly we form an important link in this divine chain.

How could the Spirit accomplish this except through redeemed human instruments?

Is Christ now in this present time receiving the witness and the glory which He deserves and indeed which He must have? Perhaps no one would be audacious enough to answer in the affirmative. If the answer is negative, what must be the cause? Is it the fault of the Spirit? Has He failed to do His appointed work? Surely not. The failure lies with us.

How often have we been more concerned about our own reputation, image, impression than we were about His? Do we seek our own glory instead of His? What does our conversation reveal? Is our "talk" about Him or of ourselves and our achievements? When we preach, are we able to recede into the background that He may have the preeminence and be exalted or do we exalt ourselves and grieve the Spirit, to say nothing of the people? Let us as individuals search out those self-loving, honor-seeking, ego-exalting obsessions and confess them before God and before our brothers.

A humble and wholesome concern for the uplifting of Christ would deliver us from much of the jealousy and malice existing among and between Christians today. And what a deliverance it would be from hurt feelings, pride, hypocrisy, deception, suspicion, backbiting, and hatred. What a mighty merging of gifts and energies, if all together we could set out on a course to glorify Christ in the power of the Spirit!

Would this not open up to us a new day of blessing and power? Would it not affect us on every level and in every relationship? Individuals, families, congregations, denominations, institutions, schools, colleges, seminaries, and publishing organizations.

All worshipers would very soon know that Christ was being exalted in the church. All readers of Christian literature would soon realize something of the writers' excitement with Jesus Christ. All students in Christian colleges and seminaries would be convinced of the professors' devotion to the Lord of the church regardless of the course being taught. May God hasten the day when the total program of the church, everywhere and in every way, will be in exaltation of the Lord of the church.

2

BORN
OF THE
SPIRIT
John 3:1-8

By David Ewert

1. When the Spirit of God began to move deeply in the life of John Bunyan in the seventeenth century, he tried to reform himself outwardly in life and manners, for he was known as a very wicked person. He was so successful that he thought he pleased God as much as any man in England; the neighbors, too, marveled at the change.

2. But in retrospect Bunyan admitted that his heart has been "unweldable" — using a figure from his trade as blacksmith. However, God's Spirit continued to work and he began to see the wickedness and deceitfulness of his heart, and for about a year he walked about smitten in conscience with no assurance of forgiveness.

3. One day he happened to walk along the street of Bedford and he came upon three or four poor women sitting at a door in the sun talking about the things of God. Bunyan says: "I drew near to talk to them, for I was now a brisk talker about religion. I heard, but I understood not; for they were far above me, out of my reach; for their talk was about a *new birth*, the work of God in their hearts."

4. In some respects Bunyan was not unlike Nicodemus in his search for answers to the deepest questions of his life and also in his bewilderment, when Jesus spoke to him about the new birth.

5. As a man of high position — a ruler of the Jews, a master of Israel, perhaps a member of the Sanhedrin — he comes to Jesus somewhat gingerly.

6. He visits Him at night: (a) That is often understood to suggest that he was afraid of his fellow Pharisees, and he may well have been fearful, for it was dangerous for a man in his position to identify with the preacher from Nazareth. In any case, he came to Jesus, and our Lord did not condemn him.

(b) Others feel that Nicodemus wanted the Master for himself; during the day this was quite impossible. Moreover, according to rabbinic teachers, the night was an excellent time to study.

(c) Since John had a tendency to use words with a "double entendre," as the French say, with a double meaning, it is possible that the word "night" is to suggest also the spiritual darkness in which Nicodemus found himself.

5. While his colleagues resented this Galilean "revolutionary," who stirred up the people, Nicodemus felt there was something about Jesus that could

not be written off or dismissed lightly; here was something that must be investigated. He had been aroused by Jesus' signs and was convinced that God was with Him (an Old Testament way of saying that a man was a prophet, Ex. 3:12; Jer. 1:19).

6. But Jesus takes Nicodemus away from all peripheral questions, and goes straight to the heart of the matter. He declines to carry on with a courteous exchange that leads nowhere. In one sentence He sweeps away everything that Nicodemus as a Pharisee stood for. To see signs and wonders is not salvation; to acknowledge Jesus as a prophet is not enough, either. "Nicodemus, you must be born again; you must be completely remade!"

I. The Fact of the New Birth

1. The terminology is peculiarly Johannine, although the concept of a new birth is not absent in other New Testament writers. First Peter 1:13 and James 1:18 say that the believers have been begotten of God; Titus 3:14 speaks of a begetting through the Holy Spirit, to mention only a few.

2. Nor is the concept of a new birth peculiar to the New Testament. (a) We are given to understand that Gentile converts to Judaism, proselytes, were described as newborn children. Jewish teachers even theorized on whether a proselyte could marry his own sister, since he was born again.

(b) The term was also used in the mystery religions where initiates were said to be born again; in Mithraism this new birth was affected by blood. So it is not the term that is unique, but the meaning of it in the mouth of Jesus.

3. Perhaps there is no metaphor in the New Testament that speaks of conversion, of repentance, of the beginning of the new life with such radicalness as that of the new birth.

4. Imagine, to have one's past blotted out, to start all over again, a complete renewal of our being, old things have passed away, behold all things have become new.

5. Jesus uses a word here (*anothen*) which can mean either (a) born again, afresh, from the beginning, or (b) born from above. "From above" may fit in better with Johannine vocabulary, but perhaps it's best to take both meanings into account — a translator, of course, must choose one or the other.

6. Jesus says to Nicodemus that unless he is born again, from above, he cannot see the kingdom of God. To see is to "experience" and so there is little difference between seeing the kingdom and entering the kingdom of God (v. 5). God's kingdom is God's reign, which was ushered in by the coming of Jesus and which will have a glorious consummation when Christ returns. Membership in God's kingdom, then, is restricted to those who are born again, whose lives are re-created and redirected.

II. *The Necessity of the New Birth* (vv. 6, 7)

"That which is born of the flesh is flesh, and that which is born of the Spirit is spirit. Do not marvel that I said to you, "You must be born anew."

1. The need for a new birth lies in the fact that the quality of our life is determined by our origin, and all of us are born "of the flesh."

2. *Sarx* here is not quite like the Pauline use of

19

flesh, where it is an evil power operating in fallen man, but it does mean that we are under the limitations of the flesh and in the end that spells doom. In any case, there is no hope of salvation from the flesh.

3. Nicodemus asks how a man, when he's old, can enter again into his mother's body and be born again — but to return to the flesh a second time would mean to be born of flesh again. It's a vertical break with the past that is needed — life from above, the gift of the Spirit, which is the principle of the new life.

4. There is no evolution from flesh to Spirit (not even growing up in a Christian family guarantees this kind of development). Flesh and Spirit in our text are not two sides of human nature, but stand for two different orders of existence. Grace does not run in the blood. There's no way in which Christian parents can give us this new life simply by virtue of being our parents.

5. For that reason Jesus said: You must (Greek: it is necessary) that you (plural) be born again. There is no way by which human nature by being religious, by spiritual discipline, by self-induced ecstasy, can emancipate itself from its fleshly order of existence. There are religions in which it is believed that salvation lies in deliverance from the flesh (Gnosticism, Hindu Sansyasin), but Jesus says there is no way in which a human being can change the order of his existence.

6. The nineteenth century had a very optimistic view of man; with widespread acceptance of the theory of man's physical evolution, went also the

theory of his moral progress. But human nature is not perfectable; man today is no better than he was 5,000 years ago. The need for a new birth is just as necessary in the twentieth century as it was when Jesus told a man of high position, known for his moral rectitude, in the first century, "You must be born again."

III. *The Means of the New Birth* (vv. 3-5)

1. Accepting the necessity of the new birth, the question then arises: But how? (v. 4). How can a man be born again, when he is old? And we might add: "Or when he is young?" — for age makes no difference.

2. Was Nicodemus hurt by Jesus' answer to his quest? He knew of Gentiles being born anew, but for a Pharisee, a great teacher in Israel — was the Rabbi Jesus not a bit rude? That would be like telling an Episcopalian dignitary to go and get converted in a rescue mission in downtown Chicago.

3. Or, did Nicodemus choose to misunderstand in order to get an even clearer answer? It would be wonderful to make a completely new beginning, but how? Jesus says: "Except a man be born of water and of the Spirit, he cannot enter into the kingdom of God."

4. We can understand that for a new life to begin, a new creation to take place, the Spirit of God must exercise His creative power (as He did at the first creation, Gen. 1:2), but why add water? (and some scholars insist that water is a later addition).

(a) Our Lord may have used it to suggest the purification of the heart. John baptized with water for repentance of sin, the One coming after him would baptize with the Spirit. If cleansing is the meaning, then perhaps a text like Ezekiel 36:25 f. underlines Jesus' words: "I will sprinkle clean water upon you, and you shall be clean . . . a new heart I will give you, and a new spirit I will put within you."

(b) Procreation — born by water is natural birth; by Spirit is spiritual. Evidently rabbis spoke of natural begetting as a begetting with water. Or, if water stands for birth, the two words put together mean "spiritual birth."

(c) Christian baptism. Whenever baptism with water and baptism with Spirit are in juxtaposition in the New Testament, water refers to John's and Spirit to the outpouring of the Spirit at Pentecost. In Christian water baptism the two are combined (e.g., Acts 19 where the Spirit transforms Johannine to Christian baptism). Here in our text they are not in juxtaposition and so the two together are taken by some interpreters to refer to Christian baptism. Of course, that does not yet mean baptismal regeneration, for the whole passage emphasizes that a new life is possible only by the power of the Spirit and not by the performance of any rite. This would have made no sense to Nicodemus.

5. My inclination is toward (a) purification, as represented by John's baptism — this would have made sense to Nicodemus, but I may be wrong. But, whatever view one holds with respect to water, the text is explicitly clear (as we read on into v. 6 ff.) that the source of the new life is the Spirit of God.

6. This, of course, is perfectly in line with Titus 3:5: "Not by works of righteousness which we have

done, but according to his mercy he saved us, by the washing of regeneration, and renewing of the Holy Ghost." Man cannot erase his past any more than he can become a baby again, but God by His Spirit can make him a new creature in Christ Jesus.

7. It is by the working of God's Spirit that our consciences are awakened, so that we see our need for a new life; it is by the Spirit that the invitation of the gospel becomes God's call to us; it is by the Spirit that we are convinced that we can trust in Christ's offer of eternal life (1 Thess. 1:5, 6); and it is by God's Spirit that we are assured of our membership in God's family. It is by the Spirit that we confess Christ as Lord (1 Cor. 12:1 ff.) and by the Spirit that we can say, "Abba, Father" (Gal. 4:5, 6).

However, God's Spirit is not under man's control, but works sovereignly and in freedom.

IV. *The Mystery of the New Birth* (v. 8)

1. The *pneuma* blows where it wills — this is another word with two meanings: wind or spirit (as is the case with Hebrew *ruach*). The context, in my view, favors wind, but either way, the blowing of the wind (or of God's Spirit) is incomprehensible.

2. When fanning mills were first introduced into Scotland, some pious folk objected to them on the grounds that the Bible teaches that the wind blows where it wills, and now man was making it blow where it didn't will. Well, that's a rather perverse use of the Bible.

3. Some scientists may tell us that the wind blows according to very rigid physical laws and doesn't blow where it wills — that kind of thinking is equally

perverse. This is popular language and makes perfectly good sense. For all we know a gust of wind may have swept through the narrow streets of Jerusalem at the very moment when Jesus and Nicodemus were closeted together. Jesus said that's how the Spirit works.

4. You don't know where the wind comes from nor where it goes, but you hear its sound, its whisper, its murmur, its howl. So the Spirit of God is beyond the control and comprehension of man. It breathes into this world from another realm; men cannot in themselves fathom the operations of the Spirit, but they are real. He breathes God's life into man and transforms human existence. It blows into the valley of dry bones and they live.

5. Today we hear the winds of God blowing in various places — revivals in various parts of the land, on college campuses (as was the case also at EMC). At times it's like a still small voice; at other times it seems to sweep through a church, a school, a community like a tornado. But it's unpredictable and incomprehensible. There have been times in history when it seemed as if the life of the church was nearly extinct and then in great freedom, God's Spirit blew upon a church, a land, a continent — in renewal and revival.

6. Although the new birth is a mysterious process like the blowing of the wind, it is a very real experience. One doesn't have to know the mysteries of an airplane in order to experience the miracle of being transferred within a few hours from "frozen" central Canada to the "beautiful" state of Virginia. Those who have experienced the new birth by the

24

Spirit witness to the reality of it.

Conclusion: Bunyan says of the womenfolk on the street of Bedford whom he heard speaking about the new birth that "they spake as if joy made them speak; they spake with such pleasantness of scriptural language and with such appearance of grace in all they said, that they were to me as if they had found a new world and my own heart began to shake as mistrusting my condition to be naught; for I saw in all my thoughts about religion and salvation the new birth did never enter my mind."

He left these godly women, sitting there on the doorstep, and went about his business, but their conversation did not leave him, for he was now convinced that he lacked the experience of the new birth. He returned several times to talk to them about it and he confesses that God gave him "very great softness and tenderness of heart."

Then it happened that he heard a sermon on Song of Solomon 4:1, "Thou art fair, my love; behold, thou art fair," and these words assured him of God's love for him. "I could believe that my sins were forgiven; I was taken up with the love and mercy of God that I could hardly contain myself till I got home. I thought I could have spoken of His love and mercy to me even to the very crows that sat on the ploughed land before me." He had been born of the Spirit. What about you?

3

THE
BAPTIZING
WORK
OF THE
HOLY SPIRIT
The Book of Acts

By David Ewert

The view that salvation is experienced in this life in two distant stages has been and is widely held although it is expressed in many different ways. On the one hand, one finds this disjointedness of the salvation experience in all those traditions where pedo-baptism (which is later followed by confirmation) is practiced.

On the other hand, in Puritanism the two-stage view of salvation was seen in conversion and then, at a time subsequent to conversion, the confirmation of sonship (assurance). In Wesleyanism the two stages of Christian experience were thought of as justification and partial sanctification at conversion, and then, at some later time, entire sanctification or Christian perfection. The view is expressed so clearly in Toplady's hymn: "Be of sin the double cure, Save from wrath, and make me pure."

Another way of expressing this "holiness" teaching is to say that at conversion we are delivered from the penalty of sin, and then, as a second divine work of sanctification, we are (at some later stage in our Christian experience) delivered from the power of sin. It used to be prominent in the Keswick emphasis on the "second blessing."

The "baptism of the Spirit" came to be associated with this second stage of Christian experience, although the term was understood in different ways. Some Puritans identified the experience of assurance as "a baptism with the Spirit." In Methodism "entire sanctification" was called by some a baptism of the Spirit. Through the influence of R. A. Torrey (in America, at least) the baptism of the Spirit came to stand not for sanctification, but for the empowering for prayer and service. About the same time, several Holiness leaders came to a new appreciation of the gifts of the Spirit, which they thought should be present in the church today (e.g., A. J. Gordon, A. B. Simpson — the latter was interested particularly in divine healing).

It was in this context that Pentecostalism emerged (Topeka, Kansas, 1900; Los Angeles, 1906), with its insistence that speaking in tongues is the outward sign that a person has received the baptism in (or with) the Holy Spirit. Three distinctive doctrines emerged out of this movement: (1) that the baptism with the Holy Spirit is a second (Pentecostal) experience distinct from and subsequent to conversion; (2) that speaking in tongues is the necessary and inevitable evidence of this baptism — it was this teaching which set the Pentecostal movement off from some other Holiness groups (e.g., C.M.A. renounced this teaching and lost many members to Pentecostalism as a result; the Church of the Nazarene parted company with Pentecostalism when the latter laid such a stress on speaking in tongues); (3) that the spiritual gifts listed in 1 Corinthians 12:8-10 may and should be manifested when Pentecostal Christians meet for worship.

Whereas Pentecostalism was less rigid in the earlier years of its history (although some of its leaders were very rigid, leading to endless proliferation of the movement into independent denominations), succeeding generations hardened these beliefs into dogmas. Today there appears to be greater flexibility again, as main-line denominations become less critical of Pentecostalism. In the past twenty years or so, there has come a widespread recognition of Pentecostalism as a kind of "third force" in Christendom (along with Catholicism and Protestantism). What is more, Pentecostal teaching has been making significant penetration into main-line denominations. And, since the Pentecostal movement has centered on the baptism in the Spirit, it has led serious students of the Scriptures to examine more closely what the Bible has to say about the baptizing work of the Spirit.

The first discovery that we make when we look for the texts that speak of the baptism of the Spirit (an expression not found at all in the New Testament) is that there are very few. Outside of the Gospels, where baptism with the Spirit is mentioned vis-a-vis John's water baptism, and where the reference is clearly to Pentecost, there are only three passages which speak of the baptizing work of the Spirit. Two of these passages are in Acts and they, like the Gospel text, refer to Pentecost. "John baptized with water, but before many days you shall be baptized with the Holy Spirit" (Acts 1:5). "And I [Peter] remembered the word of the Lord, how he said, 'John baptized with water, but you shall be baptized with the Holy Spirit' " (Acts 11:16). Both of the Acts passages, then, have to do with the coming of the Holy Spirit. The only other passage in the New Testament that speaks of the baptizing work of the Holy Spirit is 1 Corinthians 12:13: "For by one Spirit we were all baptized into one body — Jews or Greeks, slaves or free — and all were made to drink of one Spirit." This passage clearly has to do with initiation into the body of Christ, and that happens when we receive the Holy Spirit or, as the second part of the verse has it: "We . . . were all made to drink of one Spirit," i.e., at conversion, repented (Acts 2), new birth, believed, etc.

Although the term "baptism with the Spirit" is used loosely to describe different kinds of experiences in the Christian life (and we are not disparaging crisis experiences, which believers have at times found to be quite transforming), it is used correctly when applied to some second stage of our salvation experience. Baptism with the Spirit has to do with incorporation into the body of Christ. J. R. W. Stott (*Baptism and Fullness of the Holy Spirit,* p. 25) wrote: "The baptism (of the Spirit) was a unique initiatory experience; the fullness was intended to be the continuing, the permanent result, the norm. As an initiatory event the baptism is not repeatable and cannot be lost, but the filling can be repeatable and in any case needs to be maintained." And Dr. D. G. Barnhouse (*The Keswick Week*, 1948) commented: "No one may ask a believer whether he has been baptized with the Spirit. The very fact that a man is in the body of Christ demonstrates that he has been baptized of the Spirit; for there is no other way of entering the body."

In order to get an overview of what is meant by the baptizing work of the Spirit, we must look at those passages which have to do with the giving and the receiving of the Spirit. In this lecture, then, we want to take a look at the key passages in the Book of Acts to see what they say (and what they do not say) about the baptizing work of the Holy Spirit. I chose these (instead of Paul's writings) because they are crucial in this whole matter.

I. The Miracle of Pentecost (Acts 2)

A. The Day of Pentecost in Jewish Thought

1. It was the fifteenth day after Passover. This marked the end of the grain harvest, and the law prescribed that two loaves of bread were to be waved before the Lord on this day (Lev. 23:17 f.). This offering of the loaves completed the Passover sheaf offering, made on Easter Day. Of course the suggestion lies close at hand that the coming of the Spirit at Pentecost completes the first Christian Easter.

2. It was also a day of firstfruits (Num. 28:26; Lev. 23:17). The two loaves were offered as firstfruits to the Lord as samples of the harvest of grain. Whereas the firstfruits of the harvest were offered to God

at Passover in the form of a sheaf, "the real feast to celebrate the firstfruits of the harvest was the Feast of Weeks" (R. de Vaux, *Ancient Israel: Its Life and Institutions*, pp. 490 f.). We may look upon the three thousand that were initiated into the church on the day of Pentecost as a kind of firstfruits of the larger harvest to be gathered from every nation under heaven.

3. It was a day of rejoicing. The law prescribed that on the day of Pentecost offerings were to be made for the poor, and the festal joy was to be shared by all (Deut. 16:10 f.). How appropriate then that the Spirit should be given on this day, for the Spirit is a Spirit of joy. The early Christians were known for a joy that came from the Holy Spirit (1 Thess. 1:6). It is interesting that some rabbis taught that the Holy Spirit was to be found only in joyful hearts.

4. It had become the anniversary of the giving of the law. In the course of time, the Old Testament harvest festival was transformed to commemorate the giving of the law (cf. Jubilees 1:1; 6:17). Not only do the noise and the tongues of fire remind us of Sinai, but in line with the rabbinic notion that all the nations were present when God offered them the law at Sinai, so at the first Christian Pentecost representatives of all nations were present to receive God's Spirit. And as Israel was constituted "a kingdom of priests and a holy nation" (Ex. 19:6) at Sinai, so the gift of the Spirit at Pentecost creates a new people of God (1 Pet. 2:9, 10).

Suffice it to say that the Jewish background for the Pentecost festival enriches its significance for the

Christian church.

B. Attendant Circumstances of the Coming of the Spirit

1. A noise from heaven like that of a strong wind. In the Old Testament, God, whose dwelling is in heaven, often makes Himself known in the hearing of men (e.g., Gen. 3:8 f.; 1 Sam. 3:4 ff.). Also, again and again in the Old Testament the divine presence manifested itself in the wind (e.g., 1 Kings 19:11; Job 38:1). When Luke says it filled the house where they were sitting, he almost certainly alludes to Isaiah 6:4, although in the case of the prophet, the temple was filled with smoke.

The word for wind which Luke uses here is found in the Septuagint (*pnoe*) with the nuance of creative breath of God (cf. Is. 42:5, giving "[pnoe] breath to the people upon it and [pneuma] spirit to those who walk in it"). *Pnoe* carries with it the nuance of the creative breath of God, and so Luke uses it very appropriately to describe the beginning of a "new creation," the church.

2. The appearance of tongues like flames of fire. Fire is also an Old Testament symbol (among other things) for the presence of God (e.g., Ex. 3:2 ff.; 19:18) — sometimes joined with "wind" (e.g., Is. 29:6; 30:27 f.). How widely dispersed the tongues of fire were is not exactly clear. Does *pantes* (2:1) mean only the Twelve or does it include the 120? In any case the Spirit was *manifestly* given to them. Their experience was not the product of their imagination. The Spirit left His recipients in no doubt that He had come.

The fire with which Messiah was to baptize,

according to John the Baptist (cf. Lk. 3:16), is usually taken to be a reference to eschatological judgment (in keeping with the passage in Joel 2, which Peter quotes in Acts 2:19 in his Pentecost sermon). However, the passage in Luke 12:49 seems to have a different point: "I have come to cast fire upon the earth, and how I wish it were already blazing." This is connected by an adversative, *de* — "*but* I have a baptism to receive and how I am distressed until it has been completed," an obvious reference to our Lord's Passion. He can send fire (the Spirit) only after His death. The coming of the Spirit may be that fire which was cast on earth after Christ's death (cf. R. F. Zehle, *Peter's Pentecost Discourse*, p. 117).

3. They spoke in other tongues. As far as we know the phenomenon mentioned here in Acts 2:4 is different from the glossolalia in Christian worship of which Paul speaks in 1 Corinthians 14. Here it refers to the mysterious gift of communicating in another dialect. There was no great need as far as the Pentecost visitors were concerned to be addressed in their native dialects, for most of them knew either Greek or Aramaic. Rather, it seems, this miraculous gift of communicating the good news in "other tongues" was one more sign that the gift of the Spirit had been given. H. B. Swete says, "The purpose of the miracle . . . was not to lighten the labour of the Christian missionary, but to call attention at the first outset to the advent of the Paraclete" (*The Holy Spirit in the New Testament*, p. 74). We have no evidence from the New Testament that this miracle of Pentecost was repeated. Paul had the gift of glossolalia, but apparently he was not able to speak

the Lycaonian vernacular (Acts 14:8 ff.) at Lystra.

Although the ability to speak foreign languages, as on the day of Pentecost, apparently was not a permanent gift, it pointed out the church's task in history — to reverse the curse of Babel, and to let God's Word be proclaimed to man of every tongue and nation.

As a point of interest, there is a Jewish tradition which represents the voice of God at Sinai as divided into 70 voices in 70 languages so that all mankind might hear. And Rabbi Akiba declared that the voice of God was visible in flames of fire. These are interesting parallels to the Lucan account.

C. The Significance of the Pentecost Event

The promise of Jesus that the disciples would be baptized with the Spirit (Acts 1:5), that they would be equipped with power to witness (Acts 1:8), was fulfilled at Pentecost. Pentecost was a watershed in salvation history:

1. Pentecost was a sort of climax of all that had gone before. Peter in his Pentecost sermon insists that the outpouring of the Spirit was not only anticipated by David and the prophets, but was the capstone of the death, the resurrection, and the ascension of Jesus (2:29-33).

2. Pentecost signified the inauguration of the new age. The prophets had connected the dawn of the Messianic age with the outpouring of God's Spirit; that age was now here. The ascension brought to an end the story of Jesus (Luke's first volume tells that story, and his Gospel concludes with the ascension). Luke's second volume begins with the ascension, followed by the outpouring of the Spirit, the

sign that the new age had begun. The Spirit was the Spirit of promise (Acts 1:4; 2:33); the gift of the Spirit is "the blessing of Abraham" (Gal. 3:14), through whom all the nations of the earth were to be blessed. Ezekiel (36:27) and Jeremiah (31:33) had spoken of the new covenant as one in which God's law would be written into the hearts of men. This happened at Pentecost as Paul cogently argues in 2 Corinthians 3. The Spirit is the essence of the new covenant.

3. Pentecost inaugurated the age of the church, the age in which the gospel is proclaimed to the world. The church is basically a missionary body. Interestingly, we hear of no attempt on the part of the disciples before Pentecost to witness to Jesus Christ. But when the Spirit came, the world mission of the church began (Acts 1:8; 2:5). The coming of the Spirit was incontrovertible evidence that Jesus was Lord of all (Acts 2:33). Therefore, on the day of Pentecost Peter could hold out the promise to all who heard the good news: "Whoever calls on the name of the Lord shall be saved" (Acts 2:21). The list given by Luke of nationalities that formed the audience of the apostles at Pentecost stresses the universality of the gospel. Whether Luke adapted a known "geographical catalog" of nations or whether the list was original does not change the fact that the whole world was represented when the apostles proclaimed with great power the mighty acts of God on that first Pentecost. The promise is to you and to your children and to those "far off" (*eis makran*), and that is reminiscent of Isaiah 57:19, where (as in Eph. 2) it refers to Gentiles.

The Spirit is the hallmark of the church, and so

35

one can say that Pentecost is the birthday of the church. As such it is unique in the history of salvation and can never be repeated. This is the baptism with the Holy Spirit, which both John the Baptist and Jesus predicted.

But let us look at some other texts in Acts which are quite unique in their description of how the Spirit came to different people in that early period. Some of these texts are problem texts. The one that we are about to mention has been used very frequently to give scriptural support for separating conversion and a later so-called baptism of the Spirit.

II. The Samaritan Believers (Acts 8)

1. As a result of Philip's preaching in Samaria, new converts had been won. When the apostles in Jerusalem heard the good news, they sent Peter and John, who, when they arrived, prayed over the Samaritan believers and they received the Holy Spirit. If we read this account in the light of Romans 8:9, we are tempted to say that they must not have been genuine believers, since those who have not Christ's Spirit do not belong to Him. J. D. G. Dunn, in *Baptism in the Holy Spirit*, argues that the Samaritans were not genuine believers until they had received the gift of the Spirit when the apostles laid hands on them. I am not convinced by his arguments, namely, that the superstitious Samaritans had misunderstood Philip's message, that they had believed Philip (v. 12), but not in Christ; that Simon Magus also believed (and, certainly, his was not a genuine conversion); that since the Holy Spirit is the hallmark of the believer, the Samaritans can not have been genuine be-

lievers (pp. 63-67). One could also ask, then: Were the disciples genuine believers before Pentecost?

2. If the Samaritans were genuine believers, does it follow that they received the baptism of the Spirit (as Pentecostals insist)? Implied in such a view is that they had received the Spirit when they believed (something the text explicitly denies), and that they were later baptized with Spirit (something the text does not say either).

Another view is:

3. The Samaritans had received the Spirit at conversion, but the charismatic manifestations were lacking. This view founders on the explicit statement that "the Spirit had not yet fallen on any of them" (v. 16), and that the Spirit was given when the apostles laid their hands on them (v. 18). A simple exercise is to replace "Holy Spirit" in our passage with charismata, if one wants to feel how incongruous such a reading would be. The Holy Spirit, not His gifts, "falls" on people.

Still another view:

4. The Spirit is received only by the laying on of hands. We can see how this approach lends itself to give scriptural foundation to the practice of confirmation, but actually that view is fanciful. We do not read of any laying on of hands on the day of Pentecost. Even more fanciful is the view that plays into episcopalian practice, that Philip was not qualified to lay on hands and, therefore, the apostles (predecessors of bishops) had to come. Strangely, the Ethiopian eunuch was converted through Philip, baptized by him, and went on his way rejoicing. Are we to suppose that, when Ananias laid his hands on Paul, he

carried more ecclesiastical weight than Philip did? It may be amusing to think of the apostles running hither and yon to conduct "confirmation services," but highly incredible.

The best approach, in my opinion:

5. Samaria was a unique situation. Between the Jews and the Samaritans there was bitter hatred of long standing. F. F. Bruce points out, "In the present instance, some special evidence may have been necessary to assure these Samaritans, accustomed to being despised as outsiders by the people of Jerusalem, that they were fully incorporated into the new community of the people of God" (*Book of Acts,* p. 182). Lampe underscores the fact that before Samaria could be established as a nucleus for further expansion, the continuity with Jerusalem had to be established; otherwise the unity of the Spirit-possessed community would be impaired (*Seal of the Spirit,* pp. 70-72).

Perhaps the full flowering of the Samaritans' faith was delayed because they found it hard to believe that they were really accepted in the Christian community comprised so far only of Jews and proselytes. And so it was only natural that Peter and John, chief representatives of the Jerusalem church, should proffer them the hand of fellowship, so that they might come to the fullness of the faith.

The account is very brief, and Luke offers no explanations why they did not receive the Spirit immediately. The conditions for the receipt of the Spirit which Peter laid down in Acts 2:38 evidently had been met, and yet the gift of the Spirit had not been received. We are led to the conclusion that, just as Peter had opened the door of faith to the Jews, on the day of Pentecost, so he (and John) opened it now to the Samaritans (and somewhat later he opens it to the Gentiles). So we have here a kind of mini-Pentecost.

In general it should be said that in all great spiritual movements there are phenomena that can not be so easily categorized. The experience of the Samaritans seems to be of this kind. I would hesitate to say that they were not genuine believers simply because of the special manner in which the receipt of the Spirit is described. Conversely, it is precarious to argue from silence that they did receive the Spirit at conversion and that what we have here is a second work of grace. Even more precarious is to hold this story up as normative for Christian experience. How can one say that this is the pattern of Christian experience (conversion and then baptism of the Spirit — a term which, by the way, is not used in the passage), and not the experience of Cornelius, where the Spirit is received before baptism? To this story we shall turn presently, but let us take Paul's conversion next.

III. The Conversion of Paul (Ch. 9)

Some of those who look for passages on which to base the teaching of the second work of grace (or baptism in the Spirit, if Pentecostal language is preferred) insist that Paul was converted on the Damascus road and three days later was baptized in the Spirit. Others argue that Paul was merely convicted on the Damascus road and converted when Ananias ministered to him. That Paul called Jesus "Lord" then means that *kurie* is to be understood as "sir"; that Ananias called him "brother" means that he addressed

39

him as fellow Jew.

But why such fanciful divisions between what happened on the Damascus road and at the meeting with Ananias? In looking back on his experience, Paul made no distinction between the commissioning he received through Ananias (22:13 ff.) and the call directly from Christ, received on the Damascus road (26:15 ff.). The conversion-commissioning was one experience, and so was his conversion-receipt-of-the-Spirit, and baptism. A man whose loyalties to Judaism ran so deep did not have his *Weltanschauung* changed completely the moment he heard the voice from heaven. He needed a few days in which to plunge beneath the surface of all he had held dear, in order to come to an understanding of the Christian faith, of deep heart-searching and repentance — the pangs of the new *birth.* The three days of darkness remind us of the three days our Lord spent in the darkness of the grave, before the light of Easter drove the clouds away. As he called on the name of the Lord, had his sins washed away (22:16), was filled with the Spirit, and was baptized with water (22:16; 9: 17, 18), Paul became a new man in Christ.

There are three occasions in Acts where the laying on of hands and the receipt of the Spirit are connected (8:14; 9:10 ff.; 19:1 ff.). It does not follow, of course, that the laying on of hands had the same significance in each instance. Our Lord laid hands on people for healing (Mk. 5:23), and for blessing (Mk. 10:16). The apostles laid hands on the seven when they commissioned them for service (Acts 6:6).

Paul was told by the Lord that Ananias would come to him and lay his hands on him to restore his sight (as Jesus had done when He cured the blind, e.g., Mk. 8:25; Lk. 4:40; 5:13; 8:3, 4). The purpose of the laying on of hands seems to have been the recovery of sight, since it marked the last phase of Paul's conversion from darkness to light, and that was accompanied by the receipt of the Holy Spirit. In the two later accounts of Paul's conversion (22:6 ff.; 26:12 ff.), where he describes what happened to him in Damascus, there is no hint that the Spirit was imparted to him through the laying on of hands. That there was a close connection between laying on of hands, the restoration of sight, and the receipt of the Spirit can, of course, not be denied. However, it seems to be more true to the text to infer that the Spirit was given to Paul by Christ directly, without the mediation of Ananias. When Paul later insisted that he had received his apostleship not through men but from God (Gal. 1:1, 11 ff.), he is not denying a place in this experience to God's appointed servant, Ananias. As Ananias laid his hands on Paul, the power of Christ enlightened his eyes and filled him with the Holy Spirit (an indispensable qualification for apostolic service).

IV. The Conversion of Cornelius (Ch. 10)

While Peter preached to the guests who had gathered in the house of Cornelius, the Holy Spirit fell on all who heard the Word (10:44). It surprised the Jewish believers to see that the Gentiles, too, had received the Spirit (10:45). In this case there was an outbreak of glossolalia as these Gentiles came from darkness to light (10:46). The whole event is reminiscent of what happened at Pentecost when the Spirit fell on the Jewish disciples. Had these Gentile converts not spoken in tongues, the Jewish Christians present (perhaps Peter himself) would have been loath to believe that they had received the Holy Spirit.

Whereas in Acts 2:37 ff. the gift of the Spirit is mentioned after repentance, faith, and baptism, here the reception of the Spirit comes first. Indeed, faith is not even mentioned in Cornelius' story. The Spirit is poured out and they are baptized (10:47, 48). At the Jerusalem council, where Peter defended the Gentiles as bona fide members of the church, he says that they believed and had their hearts cleansed by faith (15:7-9). Be it noted, too, that the reception of the Spirit was no substitute for water baptism.

Those who try to find a gap between the conversion of Cornelius and his friends, and a later Spirit baptism, are a bit hard-pressed to find one in this account, although some insist on it even here — small though the gap may be. Such fanciful interpretations should remind us that Luke is telling the story of the progress of the gospel in the early period of the church, and that the Spirit does not always work in the same way. For we seem to have the reverse order in the case of Cornelius from what we have in Samaria — in the former case, the gift of the Spirit preceded baptism; in the latter, baptism took place before the outpouring of the Spirit. For this reason it is not proper to insist that every believer must experience what the Samaritans experienced. Why not, rather, choose the experience of the household of Cornelius? What would be the order of Christian experience, if we threw in Paul's conversion experience for good measure? The fact is that these were all unique historical events which cannot be imitated in detail because we do not stand at the turning point of the ages, as these believers and apostles did.

And what we have just said is applicable also to the experience of the Ephesian disciples — and the unique event in the history of the early church.

V. *The Disciples at Ephesus* (Ch. 19)

One of the questions which engages interpreters of this passage is: Were these former disciples of the Baptist Christians when Paul encountered them? It's a question that is not answered so easily. The designation "disciples" (v. 1) is too general to give a definite answer. Interestingly, the New English Bible has translated it "converts." There must have been many people who had had some contact with John and had received his baptism and then left the area, for we have no reason to believe that all those baptized by John were joined together in clearly marked-off communities. Paul's words to them seem to suggest that although they may have known of John's prophecy that the One coming after him would baptize with the Holy Spirit, at least they did not know of the fulfillment of that prophecy at Pentecost. (The W-text of Acts has an interesting variant here: "We have not even heard that any people are receiving the Holy Spirit.") They were still living as it were on the other side of Pentecost. The fact that they accepted water baptism a second time and received the Holy Spirit could also suggest that they were not till then genuine believers in Christ.

On the other hand, "Did you receive the Holy

Spirit when you believed? does suggest some kind of experience of the Christian gospel. Paul expressed surprise that what normally happens, namely, that a man receives the Holy Spirit when he believes, did not happen in their case. Also, the word "disciple" is the common designation for believer. But to go on from there to argue that they were baptized Christian believers, who had not yet received the baptism of the Spirit is a *tour de force*.

They may have received their knowledge of Christ from a somewhat defective source. (Could Apollos, before he was instructed by Aquila and Priscilla have been the cause of their limited understanding?) On the whole it seems better to accept the view that they were Christian believers whose faith was defective. In true Anabaptist fashion, when Paul explained to them that John's baptism was but anticipatory in character, they were rebaptized — the only account of a rebaptism in the New Testament. Whether those of Jesus' disciples (who had been disciples of John) were rebaptized at Pentecost cannot be determined with any certainty. Perhaps their Pentecostal endowment with the Spirit transformed the preparatory baptism of John into Christian baptism. Could it be that those who had received John's baptism before the death of Jesus did not need to be rebaptized, while those who were baptized by John's baptism after Christ's death (as perhaps the Ephesian disciples) were rebaptized? (F. F. Bruce asks the question, *Acts,* p. 386, n. 12).

In any case, the Ephesian disciples were baptized in the name of Jesus, and when Paul laid hands on them they received the Holy Spirit. The laying on of hands may have been part of the baptismal rite. Others feel that it symbolized the receipt of the Spirit. Still others that it was a way of commissioning them to the task of mission. Since the laying on of hands in connection with the receipt of the Spirit is mentioned only here and in Acts 8, Hull suggests that "it seems not unreasonable to conclude that reference is made to it on these two occasions only because, in Luke's view, these two cases were quite exceptional."

As in the case of the believers in Cornelius' house, the Ephesian disciples spoke in tongues. No reference is made to the proclamation of the good news in other tongues (as at Pentecost), nor does the phenomenon in these two cases seem to be what Paul describes in 1 Corinthians 14 (although that cannot be ruled out). It seems rather to refer to that strange phenomenon which at times attends the experience of those who break through from darkness to light. When men strike oil there may be fires and explosions until the new force is channeled in such a way that it can become useful for men.

To conclude in one sentence: The baptizing work of the Spirit has to do with the outpouring of the Spirit at Pentecost, the gift of the Spirit to those who believe, and their incorporation into the body of Christ.

4

THE
GIFTS
OF THE
SPIRIT
Ephesians 4:7-16

By Paul M. Zehr

This passage of Scripture sets before us the theological basis for the giving of gifts to the church. Most certainly our text refers to the humiliating death, resurrection, ascension, and exaltation of our Lord. Of particular significance in verse eight is the quotation from Psalm 68:18. The change in the quotation from "thou hast received gifts among men" to "gave gifts unto men" is worthy of our attention. The idea in Psalm 68:18 is that of a warring king returning from battle and receiving gifts for his victorious work. Archibald Hunter writes, "When the psalmist spoke of captives, he was picturing God as a conqueror marching up to the gates of a fallen city and taking tribute from the vanquished. Paul is thinking of Christ's victory over the demonic powers achieved on the cross (see Col. 2:15) and of the gifts of the Spirit which the risen and ascended Lord gave to His people." [1] The victory accomplished by Christ is shared with the church through God's gifts to the believers.

The topic "The Gifts of the Spirit" could better be entitled "Gifts of Grace," for the term "Spiritual Gifts" is seldom used in the New Testament. In 1 Corinthians 12:1 and 14:1 we have the term *pneumatikon* which is the genitive plural of *pneumatikos* meaning "spiritual things." The context led the translators to translate it "spiritual gifts," but the term "gifts" is not there in the original and is only implied by context. Not all translators render the passage "spiritual gifts." Another New Testament Greek term that brings us directly to our subject is *charismata* or gifts of grace. Paul used the term *pneumatikon* only in the Corinthian passage. Elsewhere he uses the term *charismata*. This immediately poses two questions: (1) Why didn't Paul use the term *charismata* in Corinthians as he did elsewhere? And (2) what is the difference between the terms?

A likely answer to the first question is that Paul picked up the term being used by the Corinthians. Coming from a pagan Hellenistic background, they were at home in emotional religious experiences that may have been more pagan than Christian. Paul simply starts out with their term, but in the chapter he returns to *charismata* in vv. 4, 9, 28, 31, thus relating this experience to the Christian point of view. Alone by itself, the Corinthian passage would see the terms interchangeable. But elsewhere the term *charismata* is preferred. As to the second question, it appears as if *pneumatika* is an overall term for the totality of the gifts, whereas *charismata* is the more specific term. [2]

Technically speaking, therefore, we are discussing the "gifts of grace" or the charismatic gifts. It should be pointed out immediately that a different term is used for the gift of the Holy Spirit. In Acts 2:38 Peter said, "Repent, and be baptized every one of you in the name of Jesus Christ for the remission of sins, and ye shall receive the gift (*dorea*) of the Holy Ghost." The same term used in Acts 2:38 is found in Ephesians 4:7, where the passage speaks of the gift (*dorea*) of Christ. (See also John 4:10; Acts 8:20; 10:45; 11:17; 2 Cor. 9:15; Eph. 3:7; Heb. 6:4 for the uses of *dorea*.) The difference in the Greek terms used may mean that gifts of grace and the gift of the Holy Spirit are two completely different matters. The Acts 2 setting may help clarify this for us. John R. W. Stott writes,

> The 3,000 do not seem to have experienced the same miraculous phenomena (the rushing mighty wind, the tongues of flame, or speaking in tongues). Yet they inherited the same promise and received the same gift (verses 33, 39). Nevertheless, there was this difference between them: the 120 were regenerate already, and only received the baptism of the Spirit after waiting upon God for ten days. The 3,000, on the other hand, were unbelievers and received the forgiveness of their sins and the gift of the Spirit simultaneously. And it happened immediately when they repented and believed; there was no necessity to wait. This distinction between the two companies, the 120 and the 3,000, is of great importance, because I suggest that the *norm* for Christian experience today is the second group, the 3,000, and not (as is often supposed) the first. [3]

Stott also informs us that in the interpretation of Scripture we give first attention to the didactic portions and secondary attention to the historical narratives. Simply stated, the gifts of grace, *charismata*, and receiving the gift of the Holy Spirit, *dorea*, are not the same thing. Therefore, one cannot use the test of gifts to determine if he possesses the Holy Spirit.

With the above in mind let us examine the term *charismata*. The word appears seventeen times in the New Testament. Twice it is translated "free gift" and fifteen times it is translated "gift" in the KJV. With the exception of 1 Peter 4:10, it is strictly a Pauline term. I find five different uses of the term. (See Exhibit A.)

First, is a general use as in Romans 1:11; 11:29; 1 Corinthians 1:7; 2 Corinthians 1:11. These passages indicate God's favor or graciousness to man. Second, is God's free gift of salvation to all Christian believers. The term is specifically used in Romans 5:15, 16, and in 6:23. "For the wages of sin is death; but the gift of God (*charisma*) is eternal life through Jesus Christ our Lord." Although a different term is used, the same idea is set forth in Ephesians 4:7 and 2:8, 9. Third, is God's grace in gifting groups of believers within the church. Passages such as Romans 12:6; 1 Corinthians 12:4, 9, 30, 31 belong in this category. Fourth, is God's grace in gifting individual believers as in 1 Corinthians 12:28; 1 Timothy 4:14; 2 Timothy 1: 6, and 1 Peter 4:10. Finally, in the fifth place, is God's grace in gifting a specific area of an individual's life. 1 Corinthians 7:7, the gift of celibacy, is the only listing of this charismatic gift. It may be concluded that all Christians experience God's grace in the gift of salvation. But not all believers experience the same gift of grace aside from salvation, nor does any Christian believer experience all the gifts of grace as the Greek construction of 1 Corinthians 12:29, 30 clearly implies.

There are five lists of charismatic gifts in the New Testament. (See Exhibit B.)

1. 1 Corinthians 12:8-10
2. 1 Corinthians 12:28
3. 1 Corinthians 12:29, 30
4. Romans 12:6-8
5. Ephesians 4:11

Stephen Smalley, from the University of Ibadan, Nigeria, writing in The *Journal of Biblical Literature* in 1968, made several observations concerning these lists. He writes,

> Unlike the lists in Romans 12 and 1 Corinthians 12:8-10, which refer chiefly to *charismata* as such, and that in Ephesians 4, which refers to Christians who exercise an individual gift, the two lists in 1 Corinthians 12:28-30 allude to both. But in all five cases the emphasis is undoubtedly on the corporate sharing of personal gifts by members of the *soma Christo,* rather than on the structured hierarchy of those endowed with particular gifts. [4]

Smalley calls our attention to the top of the lists where the gifts relating to the proclamation of the Word of God — apostles, prophets, and teachers — are listed first in four of the five lists. He further calls our attention to glossolalia as being listed in only three of the five lists and in each case as being found at the foot of the lists. Scholars refer us to the work of Robertson and Plummer's commentary on 1 Corinthians for these five lists. These men see 1 Corinthians 12:28, which gives the order of importance of the gifts in the church, as a guide for understanding the other lists. [5]

Additional study enables us to see a relationship within the gifts. Some complemented others. For example, the gift of teaching was accompanied by the gifts of wisdom and knowledge. The gift of faith was accompanied by the gifts of healing and working of miracles. Other gifts had a corresponding gift to hold it in check. For example, the gift of prophecy was kept in its proper place by the gift of discerning of spirits. The gift of tongues was made useful in the worship experience by the gift of interpretation of tongues. Otherwise, says Paul, it is useless in the worship service.

In the early church, some gifts were designed to aid in a traveling ministry, whereas others aided the local church setting. Westcott says,

> The three groups "apostles," "prophets," "evangelists" represent ministers who had a charge not confined to any particular congregation or district. In contrast with these are those who formed the settled ministry, "pastors" and "teachers," who are reckoned as one class not from a necessary combination of the two functions but from their connection with a congregation. [6]

The Interpreter's Bible Dictionary says,

> We are justified in inferring that the *evangelists,* on the contrary, are the missionaries of his own generation, who do not serve any one congregation or area, but move from place to place as they find openings for the proclamation of the gospel. The *pastors* and

teachers are mentioned in a way that sets them apart from the former three categories; the form of the phrase might be taken to mean that these are dual titles for a single office — reflecting the twofold task of a settled ministry, with its duties of pastoral care and instruction; or it may simply mark them out as representatives of two different offices, linked together as sharing the care of established congregations, in distinction from the three former classes, who bring new congregations into being. [7]

I would suggest that we classify the gifts according to their functional role within the church. I see three basic areas of the church's life in which the gifts are in operation. These are proclamation, service, and administration. Let us seek the meaning of each gift under these three major functional roles.

I. The Gifts of Proclamation

a. Apostles

The apostles, with the highest gift one could possess, served the church at large. Lindsay says,

> The apostles were men who in virtue of the implanted "gift" of "speaking the Word of God" and the "call" impelled them, were *sent forth* to be the heralds of the kingdom of Christ. This was their lifework. They were not appointed to an office, in the ecclesiastical sense of the word, but to a *work* in the prosecution of which they had to do all that is in the inevitable accompaniment of missionary activity in all ages of the church's history. [8]

The apostles were persons chosen individually by Christ. They were recipients of divine revelation and wrote New Testament books. At their death, the apostolic role and office ceased in the church, but some of their work of proclaiming the Word of God was continued by the evangelists.

b. Prophets

In contrast with the apostolic gift which included a traveling ministry, the prophet was generally tied to a local church setting. "While the apostle, as we have seen, was one 'sent forth' to the unbelieving world, the prophet was a minister to the believing church (1 Cor. 14:4, 22). Ordinarily, his message was one of 'edification, and exhortation, and consolation' (1 Cor. 14:3). Occasionally he was empowered to make an authoritative announcement of the Divine will in a particular case (Acts 13:1 ff.)."[9] The gift of exhortation supplemented the prophetic gift.

c. Teachers

Ability to explain and apply Christian doctrine defines the gift of teaching. It was accompanied by the gifts of knowledge and wisdom. By knowledge we mean the ability to see into man and determine what his needs are. And by wisdom we mean the ability to turn knowledge into an advantage. One writer says, "By *gnosis* [knowledge] we have an intelligent grasp of the principles of the gospel; by *sophias* [wisdom] a comprehensive survey of their relations to one another and to other things."[10]

II. The Gifts of Service

a. Ministry

Here is an overall term for the service role in the early church.

b. Faith

Robertson and Plummer define this gift as, "the

wonder-working faith which manifests itself in *erga* [works] rather than in *logos* [word]; potent faith."[11] Two additional gifts supplemented it. First, was the gift of healing which Pache has called, "the intervening of God in a supernatural way in our lives by which He heals us of any particular disease."[12] Second, was the gift of miracles which is the ability to perform supernatural acts aside from the gift of healing.

c. Helps

Again we have an overall term. We must remember, however, that these gifts were operative in the church prior to the development of long-term official offices. Some gifts eventually led to permanent offices in the church. The gift of helps is a case in point. The *International Standard Bible Encyclopedia* says, "the gift of helps appears to furnish the germ of the gracious office of the deacon — the 'minister' par excellence, as the name *diakonos* denotes — which we find in existence at a latter date in Philippi and Ephesus."[13]

d. Pastors

Like the shepherd, the pastor fed, guided, and protected the flock of God — the church.

e. Ecstatic gifts

In this group is the gift of prophecy, insight into revealed truth and a great faculty for making its consequences known, with its counter gift the discerning of spirits to keep it in balance. The latter enabled the church to detect false teaching, false prophets, etc. Finally, comes the gift of tongues, glossolalia, or ecstatic utterances as the Greek implies, with its accompanying gift, the interpretation of

54

tongues to make it useful in the worshiping assembly of believers. It should be noted in passing, there is a distinction between the glossolalia in Acts 2 and in 1 Corinthians. In Acts 2 each heard in his own language. In 1 Corinthians it was ecstatic utterances that no one seemed to understand. Consequently, Paul gave extensive teaching in 1 Corinthians 14 for its proper use.

III. The Gifts of Administration

There are two gifts which God gave to the church primarily for administrative purposes, namely, ruling and governments. Ruling seemed to be the ability to administer or superintend. Governments carried the idea of steering and piloting. Both of these gifts may have eventually led to the official powers of the presbyter or bishop office.[14]

Having examined the gifts individually, let us ask, How are they given to the church? Paul answers that question in 1 Corinthians 12:11. "All these are inspired by one and the same Spirit, who apportions to each one individually as he wills" (RSV). Beyond the gift of salvation, which is given to all Christian believers, charismatic gifts are under the sovereign control of God. He gives to the person He chooses — it is God's business whether I have a gift or not. And He gives **as He wills** — which means He may give one or several gifts. It further means He may take away a gift He has given, if He so desires. Not everyone possesses the same gift, nor does any one individual possess all the gifts of grace (1 Cor. 12: 29, 30). Other than the gift of salvation and the gift of prophecy, we are not commanded to seek all the other gifts. But we are commanded to practice love in the congregation where the gifts are in operation under God's sovereign control (1 Cor. 13). And we are not to forbid the use of a gift including the gift of tongues (1 Cor. 14:39).

Another consideration is the purpose of the charismatic gifts. In Ephesians 4 Paul explicitly states they are given to equip the saints for ministry in the world and to edify, or build up, the body of Christ to its full stature in Him. In so doing they produce unity and harmony in the church. The same kind of emphasis is found in 1 Corinthians 12 — 14. Gifts should never divide a congregation. Nor should those possessing a certain gift become a clique meeting separately from the congregation on a regular basis, whether they be persons with the gift of proclamation or persons with the gift of glossolalia! Instead, **they are to function within the central life of the people of God.** As each gift is allowed to operate in its biblical sense, harmony is produced. Let us therefore, as a Mennonite brotherhood, get on with the unity, edification, and evangelism that the gifts are intended to produce among us!

One final word of caution may be in order: Nowhere in the New Testament do I find the possession of spiritual gifts the criterion by which we are to measure anyone's depth of spirituality. Instead, our measuring rod is the person of Jesus Christ. The fruit of the Spirit, or as someone has called it — the Christ-like personality, is to be found in every believer's life. Paul tells us in Romans 8:29 we are to be conformed to the image of Christ. Aside from salvation the proper question we must face is not, What gifts

of grace do I possess or how many? But the ultimate
test question is, How Christlike am I?

Exhibit A
The Work of Grace

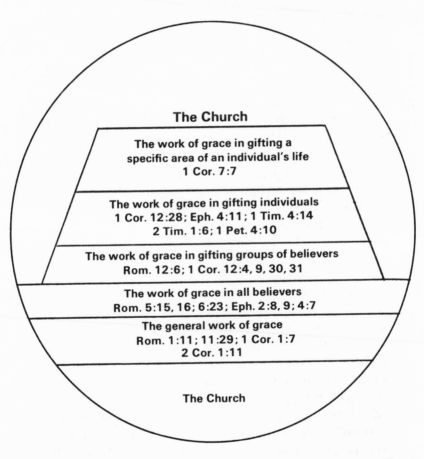

The Church

The work of grace in gifting a
specific area of an individual's life
1 Cor. 7:7

The work of grace in gifting individuals
1 Cor. 12:28; Eph. 4:11; 1 Tim. 4:14
2 Tim. 1:6; 1 Pet. 4:10

The work of grace in gifting groups of believers
Rom. 12:6; 1 Cor. 12:4, 9, 30, 31

The work of grace in all believers
Rom. 5:15, 16; 6:23; Eph. 2:8, 9; 4:7

The general work of grace
Rom. 1:11; 11:29; 1 Cor. 1:7
2 Cor. 1:11

The Church

Exhibit B

I. Five Lists of Gifts in the New Testament

1 Cor. 12:8-10
1. Spirit of wisdom
2. Word of knowledge
3. Faith
4. Gifts of healing
5. Working of miracles
6. Prophecy
7. Discerning of spirits
8. Various kinds of tongues
9. Interpretation of tongues

1 Cor. 12:28
1. Apostles
2. Prophets
3. Teachers
4. Miracles
5. Gifts of healing
6. Helps
7. Governments
8. Diversity of tongues

Rom. 12:6-8
1. Prophecy
2. Ministry
3. Teaching
4. Exhortation
5. Ruling
6. Showing mercy

Eph. 4:11
1. Apostles
2. Prophets
3. Evangelists
4. Pastors
5. Teachers

1 Cor. 12:29, 30
1. Apostles
2. Prophets
3. Teachers
4. Workers of miracles
5. Gifts of healing
6. Tongues
7. Interpretation of tongues

II. Classification According to Location

Traveling gifts
1. Apostles
2. Teachers
3. Evangelists

Local gifts
1. Pastors
2. Governments
3. Helps
4. Prophets

III. Classification According to Function

Proclamation	Service	Administration
1. Apostles	1. Ministry	1. Ruling
-evangelism	2. Faith	2. Governments
2. Prophets	-healing	
-exhortation	-miracles	
3. Teachers	3. Helps	
-spirit of wisdom	4. Pastors	
-spirit of knowledge	5. Ecstatic gifts	
	-prophecy	
	-discerning of spirits	
	-tongues	
	-interpretation of tongues	

IV. Classification According to Importance (1 Cor. 12:28)

1. Apostles
2. Prophets
3. Teachers
4. Then
     -gifts of healing
     -helps
     -governments
     -diversity of tongues

Bibliography

A. Reference Works

Abbott-Smith, G. *A Manual Greek Lexicon of the New Testament* (Edinburgh: T & T Clark, 1937).

Arndt & Gingerich. *A Greek-English Lexicon of the New Testament* (Cambridge: The University Press, and Chicago: The University of Chicago Press, 1956).

Buttrick, George A., editor. *Interpreter's Dictionary of the Bible*. Vol. IV (New York-Nashville: Abingdon Press, 1951).

Cremer, Hermann. *Biblico-Theological Lexicon of New Testament Greek* (Edinburgh: T & T Clark, Reprinted 1954).

Friedrich, Gerhard, editor. *Theological Dictionary of the New Testament* (Grand Rapids: Wm. B. Eerdmans Publishing Co., 1968).

Hunter, Archibald M. *The Layman's Bible Commentary*. Vol. 22 (Richmond: John Knox Press, 1959).

Orr, James, editor. *The International Standard Bible Encyclopedia*. Vol. V (Grand Rapids: Wm. B. Eerdmans Publishing Co., 1939).

Robertson and Plummer. *A Critical and Exegetical Commentary of the First Epistle of St. Paul to the Corinthians* (Edinburgh: T & T Clark, 1914).

Smith, J. B. *Greek-English Concordance to the New Testament* (Scottdale: Herald Press, 1965).

Vine, W. E. *An Expository Dictionary of New Testament Words* (Westwood: Fleming H. Revell Company, 1966).

Westcott, Brooke F. *Saint Paul's Epistle to the Ephesians* (Grand Rapids: Wm. B. Eerdmans Publishing Company, no date).

B. Books

Lehman, Chester K. *The Holy Spirit and the Holy Life* (Scottdale: Herald Press, 1960).

Lindsay, Thomas M. *The Church and the Ministry in the Early Centuries* (New York: George H. Doran Company, no date).

Pache, Rene. *The Person and Work of the Holy Spirit* (Chicago: Moody Press, 1954).

Ramm, Bernard. *The Witness of the Spirit* (Grand Rapids: Wm. B. Eerdmans Publishing Company, 1959).

Stott, John R. W. *The Baptism and Fullness of the Holy Spirit* (Downers Grove, Illinois: Inter-Varsity Press, 5th Printing 1971).

C. Articles.

Currie, Stuart D. "Speaking in Tongues," *Interpretation.* Vol. XIX, 1965.

Moody, Dale. "Charismatic and Official Ministries," *Interpretation.* Vol. XIX No. 2, April 1965.

Smalley, Stephen S. "Spiritual Gifts and 1 Corinthians 12-16," *Journal of Biblical Literature,* Vol. LXXXVII, 1968.

Footnotes

1. Archibald M. Hunter. *The Layman's Bible Commentary.* Vol. 22 (Richmond: John Knox Press, 1959), p. 65.
2. Gerhard Friedrich (Editor). *Theological Dictionary of the New Testament* (Grand Rapids: Wm. B. Eerdmans Publishing Company, 1968).
3. John R. W. Stott. *The Baptism and Fullness of the Holy Spirit* (Downers Grove, Illinois: Inter-Varsity Press, 1971 Printing), p. 17.
4. Stephen S. Smalley. "Spiritual Gifts and 1 Corinthians 12-16," *Journal of Biblical Literature,* Vol. LXXXVII, 1968, pp. 427-433.
5. Robertson and Plummer. *A Critical and Exegetical Commentary on the First Epistle of St. Paul to the Corinthians* (Edinburgh: T & T Clark, 1914), p. 265.
6. Brooke F. Westcott. *Saint Paul's Epistle to the Ephesians* (Grand Rapids: Wm. B. Eerdmans Publishing Company), p. 60.

7. George A. Buttrick, editor. *Interpreter's Dictionary of the Bible*. Vol. IV (New York-Nashville: Abingdon Press, 1962).

8. Thomas M. Lindsay. *The Church and the Ministry in the Early Centuries* New York: George H. Doran Company), p. 75.

9. James Orr, editor. *The International Standard Bible Encyclopedia*. Vol. V (Grand Rapids: Wm. B. Eerdmans Publishing Co., 1939).

10. Robertson and Plummer, *op. cit.*, p. 265.

11. *Ibid.*

12. Rene Pache. *The Person and Work of the Holy Spirit* (Chicago: Moody Press, 1954), pp. 180-201.

13. Orr, *op. cit.*

14. *Ibid.*

5

LED
BY THE
SPIRIT

By Fred E. Augsburger

Much has been discussed about the theology of the Holy Spirit these days in this consultation on the Holy Spirit. Numerous persons have come to me requesting that I talk now about some practical things in relation to being led by the Holy Spirit. The Holy Spirit desires to manifest Jesus Christ in more practical ways than the Mennonite Church as a whole has allowed Him to do.

To have the sense of being led by the Holy Spirit brings great assurance, confidence, and blessings to any man or woman. It releases them and sets them free to follow the Lord and minister in tremendous ways.

To be led by the Spirit we must first of all be certain that we are children of God. This is pointed out to us in Romans 8:14: "For as many as are led by the Spirit of God, they are the sons of God."

Some of the first prerequisites to being led by the Holy Spirit in effective ways is to spend much time in prayer and meditation in the Word of God. In Acts 10 we read about Peter going up on the housetop to pray. When it was nearly mealtime, he fell into a trance as he prayed. The Lord spoke to him and brought to him a vision and a message that were very vital in changing his life and that of the Christian church. The Lord called Peter to minister to people he had formerly shunned and whom he would have continued to bypass without this vision.

Fasting along with prayer is another fruitful way of being conditioned to be led by the Holy Spirit. This is also taught in the Scriptures. Isaiah 58 is a good chapter to study to learn things to do and not to do to be blessed in fasting.

With extra prying into the private lives of people who are being used in marvelous and unusual ways in the ministries of the Lord, I have discovered that, in many cases, almost half of their time is spent in fasting and praying rather than in just praying alone. In Isaiah 58 the Lord says if we will fast correctly He will guide us continually, vv. 6-11. It is wonderful to know divine guidance from the Lord continually, so fasting is a worthwhile obedience.

Praying in the Spirit will enable us to be led by the Holy Spirit. Paul wrote in 1 Corinthians 14:15, "I will pray with the spirit, and I will pray with the understanding also. . . ." He wrote in Romans 8: 26, 27 "Likewise the Spirit also helpeth our infirmities; for we know not what we should pray for as we ought; but the Spirit itself maketh intercession for us with groanings which cannot be uttered. And he that searcheth the hearts knoweth what is the mind of the Spirit, because he maketh intercession for the saints according to the will of God."

I am not ashamed to testify that I have prayed in groanings and also in unknown tongues as well as with understanding. One of the greatest lessons I have learned is that when you don't know how to deal with a person or how to pray for him, just look to the Lord and ask Him to pray through you in the Spirit. We do not always know people's problems, fears, and hang-ups which they hesitate to verbalize. Maybe they are not fully aware of their subconscious problems either. So when you pray in the Spirit, who knoweth all things, you often instantaneously see people released and set free. It is thrilling to see answers to prayers that have bypassed the understanding of your mind.

God speaks today through visions or what might be related to trances, or dreams. I recall an experience God gave me after I had received the fullness of the Spirit in my life in a special anointing: There were some persons telling me that I had not been filled with the Holy Spirit because I had not spoken in tongues. I cried out to the Lord for assurance. I wanted to know whether my theological belief, that the Spirit-filled life is not always evidenced by the gift of tongues, was correct or not. While in meetings in Johnstown, Pennsylvania, as I was praying one night after a service and before going to bed, I asked the Lord to please reveal to me what the truth really is on this matter, so I could go forth in full assurance, knowing that His blessing is upon my life in the fullness of the Spirit.

I knew that before my tremendous filling one night in August, 1962, I had felt a great need of power within my life and ministry. I had met the conditions and God had empowered me that August night. So why had others troubled me over the gift of tongues? In bed that night, I sensed I was walking in a large room. A ray of light came into this room through the ceiling. There approached a dove down this ray of light and perched upon my shoulder. It nestled up to my ear and said, "I am Jesus that baptized you with the Holy Spirit." As a Mennonite I should say, "That filled me with the Holy Spirit." When I awoke I felt a tremendous assurance that Jesus had indeed filled me to overflowing. Visions are one of the ways the Holy Spirit gives you assurance and direction.

The Holy Spirit is with us in greater ways, as we become more yielded to Him, or as someone else said, "As He gets more of us."

Another necessary factor in being led by the Spirit is that you must believe. You cannot know the fullness of God's abiding presence without really believing. I know the blessedness of ministering in series of meetings where people are believing, trusting, and expecting great things from the Lord. There God does marvelous works. I also have experienced ministering in places where people are skeptical; where they do not believe and will not enter into God's promises. They keep God from doing what He wants to do in people's lives. Believing is simply letting God do what He wants to do with you.

In the Scriptures we are asked to believe. We do

not necessarily have to understand everything. In fact there are many things about our infinite God and His ways that we finite beings cannot understand. Ecclesiastes 11:5 says "As thou knowest not what is the way of the spirit nor how the bones do grow in the womb of her that is with child; even so thou knowest not the works of God who maketh all." We are simply asked to believe, to study all we can about His ways, and to take Him at His word and go forth serving in believing faith. The experience of giving ourselves to God without first having to come to intellectually proven conclusions (and without discarding teachings we cannot prove reasonable) is necessary, if we will enter into the fullness of God's Spirit in our lives and if He will manifest His graces through us. Sometimes we are led by the written Word of God. As we are reading the Scriptures, certain words, phrases, or verses will stand out with a witness to you that God is speaking especially to you through these words.

The Spirit of God wants to lead us into various and new directions, yet according to His Word. Jesus never leads contrary to His Word. An example of this is that I can trust the vision I had in Johnstown, because God had promised in Joel 2:28, 29 that "your old men shall dream dreams, your young men shall see visions" when He pours out His spirit upon all flesh. One Sunday morning we had a new type of worship experience in our church. At the end of the service the Lord very strongly led one of our members to read Joel 2:27 and 28 as a witness that He is in our midst and that we need never to be ashamed.

In Philippians 2:5 and 13 Paul said, "Let this mind be in you, which was also in Christ Jesus. . . . For it is God which worketh in you both to will and to do of his good pleasure." One who is born of the Spirit of God and has become a new creature in Christ Jesus and is filled with the Holy Spirit can trust the Lord to speak to him through his thoughts. " . . . We have the mind of Christ" (1 Cor. 2:16). Trust God's thoughts in your mind. Begin to act upon them in faith, and you will discover that God is leading you in the particular areas He wants you to act or speak. It is always necessary to test these thoughts by the Word of God. If our ideas are from the Holy Spirit, they will agree with the principles of the Scriptures and never be contrary to them. The message which the Lord brings through the Holy Spirit may not be definitely word by word from the Bible, or it may be, but it will always agree with the Bible teachings. Try the spirits — the message which comes through your thoughts, and if you have a witness that it is God speaking, move on by faith in assurance.

New insights and leadings by the Holy Spirit must be verified by two or three witnesses. Matthew 18:16 and 2 Corinthians 13:1 tell us that "In mouth of two or three witnesses shall every word be established." Many times, in fact, usually, if it is from God, as you sense the Holy Spirit speaking to you about moving in a new direction, or as God reveals some new insight into His Word, you will soon hear several people state that same insight, or read about it elsewhere, which causes you to feel your thoughts are on the right track.

More than ten years ago I thought I heard the Lord calling me into evangelism. I replied to Him, "Oh, not me. It is impossible with me." A brother in the Lord told me about that time, that he felt God was going to call me into evangelistic work. I still insisted that I was incapable. God again told me directly that He was calling me to this area of ministry. I finally said, "Well, I can't do it. But, if You are calling me into this kind of work, You will have to send the calls and equip me with spiritual power." Soon after I yielded to God's will, I was anointed to overflowing. I never told a soul of my call nor of my promise to obey. Right after this God began to send calls to me from other congregations to preach in revival meetings for them. If you will not obey the Lord and follow Him, then do not pray for His will. He holds you to your promises and empowers you for whatever He leads you into. First Thessalonians 5:24: "Faithful is he that calleth you, who also will do it."

The Holy Spirit leads through prophecy. Prophecies and prophets are different from teachers, evangelists, pastors, etc., according to 1 Corinthians 12:8, 9, 28, and Ephesians 4:11. Prophecies may be illuminations upon the Scriptures, but also it appears from the above-mentioned Scriptures, that prophecy is something beyond the declaration of the written Word of God. It is God speaking now through Spirit-filled believers to encourage others, to instruct them as to what God wants them to do, to comfort, to warn, and to call others to repentance (1 Cor. 14:3). In the gift of prophecy the Spirit reveals things which are not perceived with our natural mind. It is an unveiling. For examples of the work of prophecy in the New Testament see Acts 8:29; 9:15, 16; 10:19, 20; 16:7 ff.; 18:9 ff.; 22:17 ff.; 27:23, 24; Galatians 2:2; 1:12, and the Book of the Revelation of Jesus Christ.

According to Joel 2:28 prophecies are to be experienced in this age of the Holy Spirit. Prophecies might come through evangelists, teachers, etc., but they can also come through other saints called of God to be a prophet at that moment for the benefit of the body of Christ. Sometimes God puts His words directly into the mouth of the prophet, as He did in Jeremiah 1:9.

Prophecy is the expressions of Christ's heart to the church. "The gift of prophecy, when disciplined by the Spirit, is a mouthpiece of God of the greatest importance to His church, for its effect often spreads far beyond the local church to the people who are reached by them. Thus where such an outpouring of this gift has taken place, congregations have again and again been filled with praise, wonder, and adoration that our Lord Jesus Christ should reveal Himself through the Spirit and come so close to them. . . . God is revealed as the Living One and glory is given to Him" (Schlink, Basilea, *Ruled by the Spirit*, Bethany Fellowship, Inc., Minneapolis, Minnesota, pp. 47, 46).

Paul did not tell the churches to read only his letters and the Old Testament to know God's will, but he urged them to desire to prophesy (1 Cor. 14:1). To prophesy is the reason women are to wear a veiling and men are to be uncovered (1 Cor. 11:4 and 5). Yet the Mennonite Church has resisted or neglected to let supernatural prophecies, other

70

than declarations of the written Word, be manifest by the Holy Spirit to reveal more of Christ's glory and will.

We are told in 1 John 4 to try the spirits, so we are to test prophecies to be sure they are Jesus' directions to us rather than just the personal thoughts of the "prophet." The gifts of wisdom, knowledge, and discerning of spirits need to be exercised. First Corinthians 14:29 says that prophets are to be judged by others and weighed by the congregation (1 Thess. 5:21). They must agree with the Scriptures. We know that Scripture verses spoken do not need to be tested as to their truth, but as to their applications.

Also we must test the prophet and not follow the words of every person who says, "Thus saith the Lord." The life of the prophet and his message must line up with Christ's character. True prophecies from the Holy Spirit will agree with the witness of Jesus and His apostles, because Jesus said in John 16:14, "He [the Holy Spirit] will take what is mine and declare it to you."

There are occasions when the Holy Spirit speaks audibly. We should not be looking for that kind of an experience, but when He does speak that way, listen to Him, thank Him and praise the name of the Lord for this. The Lord called me by name audibly one morning to get me up to pray.

The Holy Spirit leads through Spirit-filled leaders. That is one reason why administrators need to seek all the fullness of the Spirit there is possible, so that the supernatural gifts of wisdom, knowledge, and others will be in operation and so that the church can trust these leaders' suggestions and decisions with greater confidence. We also need to test the decisions of the leaders by the same tests as we are to use on prophecies.

The Holy Spirit leads in the supernatural gifts. Every person, even ungodly ones, have natural abilities. But I am speaking about the charismatic gifts which are manifested only through the supernatural power of God, and the Lord directs. He will give each of us as laity as well as to the ordained persons, the gift or gifts that He wants us to have, and according to the needs of the body among whom we are ministering.

It is blessed for God to reveal to you the spiritual and physical needs in an audience that needs ministering to. He reveals these by the gift of knowledge so you can speak forth. When you reveal that God wanted you to call out these needs, it gives the needy persons courage to respond in faith and to be released from their difficulties. We are living in days when multiplied tensions, frustrations, anxieties, nervousness, and lots of other things are holding people in bondage. We need to have ministries today that have the wisdom and power of the Holy Spirit to see people set free. Until these people are set free, they will never be able to witness for and serve the Lord. When their needs are called out, they become aware that Jesus is really alive and deeply interested in them personally. When they respond to His love and call, they become free in the Spirit and can walk in deeper fellowship and service.

You may be wondering how the Lord reveals

needs. The Holy Spirit does this in various ways by the gift of knowledge. It can be in your thoughts. He might even reveal to you by sight and thoughts the very person who has that need. Jesus lays symptoms of physical ailments within. I feel pains at the spots of need. The Holy Spirit simply makes me know the pain or pains are not my own. I trust the Lord and speak forth what God has revealed to me. In some congregations I resist calling out the needs for fear of that group's attitudes. In such places, invariably, afterwards people will come up asking for prayer for the very ailment God had revealed to me. Sometimes it is a day or two later before they will mention their desperate need. God seems to say to me then, "I told you so. Why did you not obey My leading?"

There have been occasions when I have called out needs, but no one would respond right then. Afterwards people came up and admitted they had those needs, but would not come openly before the congregation. They begged me to pray for them now. In one community when no one responded to a call given by divine revelation, a man, present that very night, died shortly afterward of that very illness. God had wanted to heal him, but he would not respond in faith.

I do not know exactly why God wants to work by revealing needs in this way. I do know that when He manifests His power and knowledge in miraculous ways, to His glory and praise, faith is stirred up in a special charismatic way (1 Cor. 12:9). People realize God is alive. He is real and working today. If we respond to His leading, He can work supernaturally in our lives as well as in the lives of others.

In the spring of 1971, at Maple Grove Church near Atglen, Pennsylvania, the Lord revealed a definite need for healing of heart trouble. Then He further revealed through my thoughts that there was someone there needing healing from spiritual heart trouble as well as physical. When I declared this openly, a man came for prayer for both kinds. Another person stood up and confessed sin and his need of spiritual heart healing. The local pastor said to himself that if this is really of the Lord, then the person who desperately needed the heart physical healing the most, had not come up yet. She was a nineteen-year-old young lady due for open heart surgery. The pastor prayed that if this was of the Lord, then let this girl be healed. At that instant, not knowing about Melville Nafziger's challenging prayer, I declared by the revelation of the Holy Spirit, that there was still someone else whom God wanted to heal of heart trouble. Young friends began pushing this young lady towards me at the altar crying, "Here she is!" The Lord touched her as we prayed for her. To my knowledge, she has not had to have that open-heart surgery. She has been to doctors for verification of healing also.

God can do tremendous things if we are willing to believe and act upon His revelations. The trouble is, there are too many unbelieving "believers" in our midst today who are not really open to how and when God wants to minister to or through them. They have reservations against new ways — ways different from those which have been customary in their congregations. It is only as we yield to the Holy Spirit in simple and seemingly foolish obedience that we can experience His leading in the supernatural, that is the charismatic ministries. The gifts of the Holy Spirit are not intellectually explainable by the natural man. "The natural man receiveth not the things of the Spirit of God . . . because they are spiritually discerned" (1 Cor. 2:14). Leaders need to encourage Spirit-filled people to walk on with the Lord by faith in the charismatic gifts bestowed by the Holy Spirit.

God leads us only when we have fear and respect for the Lord Jesus Christ and are willing to follow and obey. Psalm 25:12 says: "What man is he that feareth the Lord? him shall he teach in the way that he shall choose." Also in verse 14 the psalmist says, "The secret of the Lord is with them that fear him. . . ." It is as we are willing to do His will that He will reveal to us through the Holy Spirit the true understanding of the Word of God. In John 7:17 Jesus says, "If any man will do his will, he shall know of the doctrine."

There is great peace when the Holy Spirit verifies that we are on the beam in our following Him. We can move forth freely then in His service with assurance that "we have the mind of Christ" (1 Cor. 2:16).

To say that we cannot experience the supernatural gifts of the Holy Spirit operating in our lives today, when Satan is very active counterfeiting these gifts (see Mt. 7:22, 23; 24:24; 2 Thess 2:9; Rev. 13:13; 16:14; 19:20); to say that we dare not as children of God trust His Spirit to lead us and to use us supernaturally, is simply to make God less than Satan. But the Bible says "Greater is he that is in you, than he that is in the world" (1 Jn. 4:4). It is tremendous to see Christ manifest His resurrection power (Eph. 1:18-20) within yourself and in others as we walk in close fellowship and obedience with Him.

Jesus leads us by circumstances — by open and closed doors.

Special anointings come as we yield wholly for the Holy Spirit to lead us in ministering to others. Sometimes we have to launch out by faith before the anointing comes. Then the anointing seems to be a witness that we are on the right track. It brings greater release of faith and obedience. You can't steer a car unless it is moving; so we must begin moving out by faith and trust the Lord to steer us onward.

All that is done through us is to bring honor and glory and praise to Jesus Christ and to the Father. We read in John 14:13 and 14, "And whatsoever ye shall ask in my name, that will I do, that the Father may be glorified in the Son."

The Lord leads us when we are praising Him. When Elisha wanted a message from the Lord, he called for the minstrel to come and play. Then the Lord spoke. I believe that if we as people of God would learn how to better adore, praise, worship, and thank the Father through Jesus Christ and His Holy Spirit, God would come in new and marvelous ways to make His will and work clearly known to us. He would lead us in ways that we have not experienced before. To know the leading of the Holy Spirit means we should spend more time in praise, thanksgiving, and worship of the Lord Jesus Christ.

One of the things that hinder the miraculous leading of the Holy Spirit in our corporate meetings is that they are structured too closely and too short of time. We do not give God an opportunity to break in and do what He wants to do. Yes, it is true that we pray for divine guidance in preparing the order of a worship meeting, but between the time that we prepare and the time of the meeting, some different needs might come in. On a recent Sunday morning, I experienced this need of change to the moment's needs, as I have many times. I had taught the prepared lesson from the Scriptures about ten minutes, when one of the sisters in the Lord cried out, "I have a great need for prayer this morning. In fact, I left home walking to sign myself into the mental hospital. I need help!" The thing to do at that point was to stop teaching the Bible lesson and to teach her how to break through to deliverance, healing, and victory and to minister to her. The Sunday school class gathered around her, laid hands on her and prayed that she might be set free from her reactions to her alcoholic husband and that she might enter into the joy of the Lord for her strength. That is what happened. We need to be sensitive to needs around us. Many times we need to stop what we are doing and obey what He is directing us to do otherwise.

In the past year I came upon a passage of Scripture in Ezekiel 47 which I think sets forth a beautiful illustration of how we are as a church and of where Christ desires to lead us. I have been accused of using this passage incorrectly. But, when the Lord brings a new application to you out of His Word, I think it is wonderful and you have a right to be blessed by this application. Since the Holy Spirit gave this application to me, several ministers have shared this same new insight and I have very recently read it in a Christian paper. Thus this application has been verified by two and three witnesses.

There in chapter 47, Ezekiel had a vision of water coming out of the side of the altar — the place of repentance. It was a very shallow flow of water at the altar. God led Ezekiel out through the water a thousand cubits to where the water was ankle deep. Again He led Ezekiel a further thousand cubits and there the waters were to the knees; through still another thousand cubits to where the waters were to the loins. At the end of the next thousand cubits, the waters became a river that could not be waded through, but could only be swum through.

Too many Christians are loafing around the altar all the time at the place of their initial experience — only talking about and resting in their salvation experience — the foundation things mentioned in Hebrews 6:1, 2. We need to move out from the altar experience: "let us stop going over the same old ground again and again, always teaching those first lessons about Christ. Let us go on instead to other things and become mature in our understanding as strong Christians ought to do" (from *Living Letters*).

As a very young child I used to go swimming in water about ankle deep. Any more water would have been too much for me, as I did not know how to swim. As I got older, I went out into knee-deep water and later to hip-deep water. Now I want water over my head to swim in.

God wants us to live in the full flow of the Holy Spirit where He buoys us up and where we must hang onto His anchor, the line of which connects

78

us with God Himself behind that sacred curtain of heaven (Heb. 6:19, *Living Letters*).

There is an opposite full flow also. Phillips translates Ephesians 2:2 thus, "Drifting on the stream of this world's ideas of living." We are not to drift in that stream, but are to swim with effort or hang on to the anchor of hope (Heb. 6:18, 19).

Everywhere that the water of the Spirit flows, according to Ezekiel 47:8, 9, 12. As there were trees along the side of the river of Ezekiel's vision, "the fruit thereof . . . for meat and the leaf thereof for medicine," so in the blessed fullness of the Holy Spirit you will partake of the fruit of the Spirit and the gifts will be manifested for healing etc. Both of these are to be in operation in our lives as we follow Jesus Christ in the full flow of the Spirit.

Along the sides of this river were miry places and marshes — places where just a little water had gotten in, but not enough water to be a blessing. Nothing lived there, as it was too salty. Nothing was healed there either. Too many people are marshes today — they have had only a trickle of the work of the Holy Spirit at the altar experience, but are good for nothing without the full flow of the river. I fear there are many people within the church membership who have not even entered into the trickle of the water, because they have not really been born again. They need the altar experience of the new birth before they can be led of the Spirit of God into the flow of the Spirit.

Jesus said, "If any man thirst, let him come unto me, and drink" (Jn. 7:37-39). The Word of God is a very effective agent in our being led of the Spirit.

When the reading and meditating of the Word is low we get cooled off and God cannot easily direct us. It is similar to the furnace boiler in our church in Youngstown. There is an automatic switch on it that kicks off and the fire goes out when the water gets too low. Then there is no heat. When the Word gets too low in our lives the fire goes out too and there is no heat, or blessing to others. When we return to fasting, praying, yielding wholly to God, and allow His Word to become an effective part in our lives, we feel a fresh inflow of the fullness of the water of the Spirit and the blessedness of being led by our Lord Jesus. There is no greater blessing than serving the Lord in the assurance that He is leading us step by step through His Spirit for His glory and praise.

6

THE
ANABAPTIST
PERSPECTIVE
ON THE
HOLY SPIRIT

By J. C. Wenger

Introduction

We now have a number of major writers in early Anabaptism to whom we can turn in the study of a topic such as this one on the Holy Spirit. The writings of Conrad Grebel, Felix Manz, and many others are rather limited in extent, but those of Marpeck (in German) and of Dirk and Menno are rather substantial. Of the latter three, Menno is undoubtedly the most gifted writer and perhaps also the best interpreter of initial Anabaptism. It is to him that we will turn in today's topic.

Many years ago Principal J. B. Smith remarked that of all the leading reformers it was Menno who wrote most about the Holy Spirit. There is, said Brother Smith, about one reference to the Holy Spirit per page in Menno. After going through the *Complete*

Writings of Menno I concluded that the Smith figure was perhaps even low. I would estimate that there are about 1,500 references to the Holy Spirit in Menno's writings.

I. Who Is the Holy Spirit?

For a variety of reasons, no Anabaptist ever wrote a treatise on systematic theology. We have to look, therefore, for some occasion in the life and service of Menno which would have led him to comment on the Holy Spirit. That occasion was provided by the doctrinal confusion and error of a fellow-minister named Roelof Martens who became a sort of sixteenth-century Arius; Martens could not bring himself to believe in the full deity of Jesus Christ. Menno and others labored patiently and yet strenuously with Martens, but failed. In 1547 they had to expel him from the brotherhood. Dirk wrote a long poem on the Father, Son, and Holy Spirit, in an attempt to safeguard the brotherhood against the views of Martens, and Menno wrote a treatise, *Confession of the Triune God*. After writing about the Father, and about the Son, Menno turned to consideration of the Holy Spirit.

> We believe and confess the Holy Ghost to be a true, real, and personal Holy Ghost, as the fathers called Him; and that in a divine fashion, even as the Father is a true Father and the Son a true Son. Which Holy Ghost is a mystery to all mankind, incomprehensible, ineffable, and indescribable . . . with His divine attributes, proceeding from the Father through the Son. . . .
>
> And the reason we confess Him to be such a true and real Holy Spirit is because we are brought to this

by the Scriptures. . . . We are baptized in His name. . . . He is a dispenser of the gifts of God. . . . He guides us into all truth. . . . He cleanses, sanctifies, reconciles, comforts, reproves, cheers, and assures us. . . . The Holy Spirit . . . adorns us with His heavenly and divine gifts . . . frees us from sin, gives us boldness, and makes us cheerful, peaceful, pious, and holy. . . . We believe and confess . . . the Father, the Son, and the Holy Ghost (which the fathers called three persons, by which they meant the three, true, divine beings) are one incomprehensible, indescribable, Almighty, holy, only, eternal, and sovereign God (*Complete Writings of Menno Simons*, pp. 495, 496).

Spirit and Word. The most common association in Menno is that of the Spirit and the Word. Literally hundreds of times he associates them. Menno saw the Holy Spirit active in the giving of the divine Word. Whatever is in the Word is there by the inspiration of the Spirit. Menno calls the Word the "true witness of the Holy Ghost and criterion (*rechtanoer*) of our consciences" (p. 89). As to that which is unclean, "Touch not, says the Spirit of God . . ." (p. 182). He calls the Scriptures "the revealed and infallible Word and testimony of the Almighty Father," and goes on to rebuke the disobedient for rejecting "His Spirit, Word, and example [that is, of Christ]" (p. 216). The Holy Spirit of God "has abundantly testified" through Paul and John that unconverted sinners will not inherit the kingdom of God" (p. 301).

II. Five Major Emphases

1. *Repent: turn from all sin.* "If you wish to be saved, by all means and first of all, your earthly,

carnal, ungodly life must be reformed. For it is naught but true repentance that the Scriptures teach and enjoin upon us with admonitions, threatenings, reprovings, miracles, examples, ceremonies, and sacraments. If you do not repent there is nothing in heaven or on earth that can help you. . . . Wherever true repentance and the new creature are not (I speak of those who are of the age of understanding) there man must be eternally lost; this is incontrovertibly clear" (p. 92). See also pp. 53, 89, 96, 361, 362, 394-405.

2. *Seek Christ and His salvation.* On one occasion Menno upheld the malefactor on the cross as a good example to follow. Penitent people "turn to Christ by the power of faith with all their hearts . . . and confidently seek His grace and mercy" (p. 376). We do not drift into the kingdom, nor do we get there by "sacraments."

" . . . We must hear Christ, believe in Christ, follow His footsteps, repent, be born from above; become as little children . . . in malice; be of the same mind as Christ, walk as He did, deny ourselves, take up His cross and follow Him . . ." (p. 101). Furthermore, we had better come to Christ when God implants such desire in us, for we cannot come "whenever it suits" us (p. 373).

3. *Yield to the Lord.* Make Christ the Lord of your life! In a writing addressed to the magistrates Menno discusses "what a genuine Christian looks like." He says, "They are people who in their weakness desire to obey the Lord's holy will . . . and heartily wish to die to all that is contrary thereto. They fight bravely against all vain and erring thoughts.

. . . (They are) persons who are prepared to take up the cross. . . . In a word, they are such as are Christ-minded, are in Christ, and Christ in them, who are led by His Spirit . . ." (p. 527).

4. *Obey the Word of the Lord.* Do whatever the holy Scriptures demand. "If you believe rightly in Christ . . . then manifest it by your lives that you believe" (p. 97). "All the truly regenerated and spiritually minded conform in all things to the Word and ordinances [regulations] of the Lord. Not because they think to merit the atonement of their sins and eternal life. By no means. . . . Oh, no, it is grace, and will be grace to all eternity. . . . A truly believing Christian is thus minded, that he will not do otherwise than that which the Word of the Lord teaches and enjoins . . ." (pp. 396, 397).

5. *Trust in Christ, and only in Him.* The Christian does not trust in law, nor in works, nor in sacraments, and not even in special dreams and visions. His whole trust and confidence are in Christ, his Savior and Lord. "We teach with Christ and say, Believe the gospel. That gospel is the blessed announcement of the favor and grace of God to us, and forgiveness of sins through Christ Jesus. Faith accepts this gospel through the Holy Ghost . . . and with the whole heart casts itself upon the grace, Word, and promises of the Lord . . ." (p. 115).

"There is none that can glory in himself touching this faith, for it is the gift of God. . . . Happy is he to whom God gives this gift. . . . He that receives it receives Christ Jesus, forgiveness of sins, a new mind, and eternal life" (p. 116). Also, there is but one remedy for sin: "Christ and His merits, death, and blood" (p. 130).

III. Doctrine of Salvation

The saved status of children. We will never understand Menno's doctrine of either baptism or salvation until we are clear on the status of children. Menno saw Israelitish children as in the saved covenant people, not by virtue of any ceremony, but through the gracious covenant of the Lord. For boys the Lord prescribed a ceremony; for girls, no ceremony. Both boys and girls were saved by virtue of God's holy and gracious covenant. So it is in Christ, only in the new covenant no ceremony is prescribed for either boys or girls.

> Little children and particularly those of Christian parentage have a peculiar promise which was given them of God without any ceremony, but out of pure and generous grace, through Christ Jesus our Lord, who says, Suffer little children, and forbid them not, to come unto me; for of such is the kingdom of heaven. Mt. 19:14; Mk. 10:14; Lk. 18:16. This promise makes glad and assures all the chosen saints of God in regard to their children or infants. By it they are assured that the true word of our beloved Lord Jesus Christ could never fail. Inasmuch as He has shown such great mercy toward the children that were brought to Him that He took them up in His blessed arms, blessed them, laid His hands upon them, promised them the kingdom of heaven, and has done no more with them [no ceremony]; therefore such parents have in their hearts a sure and firm faith in the grace of God concerning their beloved children, namely, that they are children of the kingdom, of grace, and of the promise of eternal life through Jesus Christ our Lord . . . and not by any ceremony . . . (p. 280).

Menno states over and over that children are in the kingdom (e.g., p. 133), and should even be thought of as in the church (pp. 136, 698, 700, 708). See p. 707 for Menno's confidence that even the children of unbelievers are saved.

The new birth. Regeneration is in the Scriptures ascribed, says Menno, to the Spirit and the Word (pp. 60, 75), to water and the Spirit (p. 111), and to faith and the Spirit (p. 123). In every case the Holy Spirit is God's agent of the new birth. Menno wrote a whole book on the new birth (pp. 89-102), and refers to it in various other of his writings. For example, he seems to be fond of Titus 3:5: that God saved us by the washing of regeneration and the renewing of the Holy Ghost (p. 264, e.g.). He defines the new birth as "the heavenly, living, and quickening power of God in our hearts which flows forth from God, and which by the preaching of the divine Word, if we accept it by faith, quickens, renews, pierces, and converts our hearts, so that we are changed and converted . . . from the wicked nature of Adam to the good nature of Jesus Christ" (p. 265). "We cannot be led to this godly gift of faith and of regeneration otherwise than by the Word of God through the Holy Spirit" (p. 271). Menno insists on the reality of this supernatural ministry of the Spirit: He opens our eyes (p. 70), and enlightens us (pp. 188, 328).

The baptism of Christ. Menno has much to say about our anointing (506, 818), the anointing of God (57), the Lord's unction (140, 965), the inward unction of God (301), and being anointed by the Holy Ghost (990). He tells us of our absolute need to be baptized with the Holy Spirit (123), of our need to be baptized with the heavenly fire and the Holy Ghost (125). This baptism is "the baptism of Christ" (394). Menno holds that (1) regeneration, (2) putting on Christ, and (3) receiving the Holy Ghost are "one and the same thing" (134). The church of Christ is "made up of true believers, broken in their hearts with the mill of the divine Word, baptized with the water of the Holy Ghost, and with the fire of pure, unfeigned love made into one body" (p. 145). Menno insists that "the rightly baptized disciples of Christ [are] they who are baptized inwardly with Spirit and fire, and externally with water . . ." (p. 198).

The teaching office of the Spirit. Menno speaks of those who in their hearts know the truth of God, and this truth, he says, "is known to none except those who are taught of the Spirit of the Lord" (p. 106). Divine wisdom cannot be learned in colleges, but must come down from above and be learned through the Holy Ghost (p. 107). We are able to find this great treasure, "the true knowledge of the kingdom of God," only through the Spirit (p. 326). It is the Holy Spirit who takes the truth of God's Word — which He Himself originally inspired — and makes it live in our hearts and minds.

The Spirit brings Christian assurance. In his treatise on the *New Birth* Menno describes Christians as having been "baptized with the Holy Ghost into the spotless, holy body of Christ. . . . They put on Christ and manifest His spirit, nature, and power in all their conduct. . . .

"Their hearts are heavenly and new; their minds peaceful and joyous. They seek righteousness with all their might. In short, they are so assured in their

88

faith through the Spirit and Word of God that they are victorious . . . over all bloody, cruel tyrants, with all their tortures, imprisonments . . . executions, racks, and wheels" (p. 93). Cf. 95 and 357.

The Holy Spirit makes believers inwardly beautiful. This involves being made Christlike, possessing the fruit of the Spirit. This produces true beauty of character. Menno stresses especially a broken and contrite heart. He calls the Lord's kingdom, "the kingdom of all humility," and in that realm it is not the outward adorning of the body which is sought "but the inward adorning of the Spirit" (p. 17). (There is no way to determine with certainty whether Menno's emphasis here is on the human spirit which is beautified, or whether it is the divine Spirit which effects the inner beauty of the spirit.) But in another exposition of the same point Menno is wholly clear: "You are also priests, sanctified of God, not with the external oil of Aaron and his sons, nor with the perishable blood of oxen and sheep, nor with any beautifully wrought garments of gold, silk, or precious stones as the law required. But you are anointed, sprinkled, and beautified with the oil of the Holy Ghost, the blood of Christ, and the garment of righteousness . . ." (p. 326). Menno dared to assert that even a theological opponent such as Jelle Smit ("Faber") could see and feel "the sanctification and power of the Holy Spirit in our people" (p. 760).

In a beautiful paragraph Menno tells us who it is for whom he writes: "Those I serve who with an impartial, renewed, and Christian mind allow themselves to be instructed by the Holy Spirit, the fear of God and pure love, men who have received the Lord's holy

Word and truth in [a] pure mind, who obediently follow it through the received unction, and so are free from all bitter partisanship, vain honor, hatred, and envy. For with such we find the lovely spirit of peace, a pious and sincere disposition, an unleavened, pure heart and love, and therefore also an upright and pure mind, and an unspoiled, saving position and exposition. These live no more unto their self-seeking flesh, but unto Christ and their neighbors. They subject themselves to all men, are humble, opposed to all unscriptural contention and strife; they readily acknowledge their shortcomings wherein they have erred. They make peace with their neighbors . . ." (pp. 965, 966).

The saints of Christ are partakers of the Holy Spirit. Menno was fond of figures of speech. And so he is not content to say that believers receive the Holy Spirit and are baptized by Christ with the Holy Spirit (p. 920). He says that the Lord gives them "to drink of the waters of Thy Holy Spirit" (p. 74). The Lord's Supper was especially precious to Menno. He exclaims: "Oh, delightful assembly and Christian marriage feast, where no gluttonous eating and drinking are practiced . . . but where the hungry consciences are fed with the heavenly bread of the divine Word, with the wine of the Holy Ghost, and where the peaceful, joyous souls sing and play before the Lord" (p. 148). In contrasting our pre-conversion state with our status in Christ Menno wrote: "But blessed be the Lord, now we are washed, now we are sanctified, now we are justified in the name of our Lord Jesus Christ, through the Spirit of our God. 1 Cor. 6:11. In a word, we are converted to the true

Shepherd and Bishop of our souls, Jesus Christ, who pastures us now in the rich pastures of His truth, feeds us with the bread of His Word, sustains us with the tree of life, and quenches our thirst with the water of the Spirit once more. Who can comprehend and relate this grace" (p. 327)?

The Holy Spirit makes us glad and joyful and fills us with divine love. In describing our conversion to Christ, Menno explains that "Such persons are first inwardly baptized with the Spirit and fire, according to the Word of God, are taught in the hearts by His Spirit, and are led in all divine truth, righteousness, obedience, and evangelical fruits and works. They are inwardly fired by this fire of love. . . . They embrace without reservation, continuing glad in the Holy Spirit, not only the outward baptism, but also all the works of love and the fruits of righteousness which the true mouth of the Lord Jesus Christ has taught and commanded us in His holy gospel, either Himself or through His holy apostles" (p. 246). "They become confident, satisfied, and joyful in the Holy Ghost. They get a joyful spirit, and so are made to belong to the Head and Savior. . . . They are of one heart, one soul, and one spirit with Him; they think, speak, and live, in their weakness, as He has taught and commanded them in His Word" (p. 341).

"Love is the total content of Scripture. . . . The property and fruit of love is meekness, kindness. Love is not envious, not crafty, not deceitful, not puffed up, nor selfish. In short, where love is, there is a Christian" (p. 917).

Sin grieves, even quenches, the Holy Spirit. "Some cry nothing but grace, Spirit, and Christ, but trample daily on Thy grace, grieve Thy Holy Spirit, and crucify Thy Son with their vain carnal life . . ." (p. 68). Menno said that thus did he himself live prior to his conversion — which took place in 1535 (p. 73). Menno frequently speaks of "grieving the Spirit," that is, such is the result of a life of sin (pp. 150, 196, 318). To persist in sin is to "quench" the Spirit (p. 185).

Christ's disciples secure in Him. The state churchmen of the sixteenth century actively urged the state to suppress Anabaptism by force. This occurred in Roman Catholic, Anglican, Lutheran, and Reformed lands. Menno bitterly lamented such clerical agitation, calling such persons "men of blood" (p. 939), and such doctrine "blood-doctrine" (pp. 779, 780). But of one thing Menno was certain: Christ and His Spirit were abundantly able to carry such persecuted and harassed saints through to final victory, even over death. In commenting on Christ as the foundation of His saints, Menno wrote: "All who are built upon this ground will not be consumed by the fire of tribulation, for they are living stones in the temple of the Lord. They are like gold, silver, and precious stones and can never be made to collapse (*omgestooten* — to topple) by such gates of hell as false doctrine, flesh, blood, the world, sin, the devil, water, fire, sword, or by any other means, no matter how sorely they are tried. For they are founded on Christ, confirmed in the faith, and assured in the Word through the Holy Ghost [so] that they cannot be deflected (*afkeeren* — sidetracked) from the pure and wholesome doctrine of Christ by all the furious and bloody Neros under heaven. . . . They are not to be diverted from an unblamable and pious life which is of God. . . . They are as immovable as Mount Zion . . . valiant witnesses of Christ. They have fought unto death and do so daily still (God be praised eternally). I speak of those who have the Spirit and Word of the Lord" (pp. 329, 330). Menno placed much stress on the baptism or anointing or unction of the Holy Spirit which Christ gives to those who repent and believe. (See especially pp. 57, 93, 99, 125, 140, 198, 221, 246, 247, 271, 283, 301, 304, 326, 328, 341, 396, 415, 479, 481, 506, 558, 564, 590, 732, 818, 904, 920, 924, 965, 971, 986, 990, 992.) By the "baptism of Christ" we are baptized into the body of our Lord, His holy church (pp. 415, 558). See also Menno's discussions of believers falling into private sins, known only to themselves and God (pp. 411, 412, 978, 979, 1010, 1044, 1062, 1064).

IV. Menno's Own Testimony

Prior to conversion. " . . . I am not worthy to be called Thy servant; for from my youth I served not Thee, but Thine enemy the devil with diligence" (p. 66). "I resisted in former times Thy precious Word and Thy holy will with all my powers, and with full understanding contended against Thy manifest truth, taught, and lived, and sought my own flesh, praise, and honor, more than Thy righteousness, honor, Word, and truth; nevertheless Thy fatherly grace did not forsake me, a miserable sinner, but in love received me, converted me to another mind, led me with the right hand, and taught me by the Holy Spirit until of my own choice I declared war upon the world, the flesh, and the devil, and renounced all my ease, peace,

glory, desire, and physical prosperity and willingly submitted to the heavy cross of my Lord Jesus Christ . . ."
(p. 69). (This latter quotation seems to refer to his
renunciation of Roman Catholicism, which took place
on or about January 30, 1536, and to his reception
into the Frisian Anabaptist Brotherhood led by such
men as Obbe and Dirk Philips.) "O dear Lord, I did
not know myself until I viewed myself in Thy Word.
And then I confessed my nakedness and blindness, my
sickness, my native depravity, and with Paul I
realized that in my flesh dwelt no good thing. . . .
Nothing I did was done without sin. O Lord, remember
not the sins of my youth, committed knowingly and
unknowingly so oft before Thee, nor my daily
transgressions in which because of my great weakness
I am alas found daily . . ." (p. 70).

   "O sovereign Lord, Thy divine grace has shone
around me, Thy divine Word has taught me, Thy
Holy Spirit has urged me, until I forsook the seat of
the scornful. . . . I was wicked and carried the banner
of unrighteousness for many years. I was a leader in
all manner of folly. . . . I was a lord and prince in
'Babylon.' . . . The world loved me and I it" (p. 71).
"And yet the deeper I am grieved, the more I am
consoled by Thy Word, for it teaches me Thy mercy,
grace, and favor, and the remission of my sins through
Christ. . . . This promise quiets me. This promise
gladdens me . . ." (pp. 77, 78). Menno recognized the
special help God gave him to renounce the Catholic
Church and his priesthood: "After [preaching Evangelical doctrine in his Catholic pulpit] about nine
months or so, the gracious Lord granted me His
fatherly Spirit, help, and hand. Then I, without con-

straint, of a sudden, renounced all my worldly reputation, name, and fame, my unchristian abominations, my masses, infant baptism, and my easy life, and I willingly submitted to distress and poverty under the heavy cross of Christ..." (p . 671).

Ever unworthy. "But I repeat, I am a poor, miserable sinner who must daily fight with this flesh, the world, and the devil, and daily seek the mercy of the Lord, and who with the holy Paul boasts of nothing but Christ Jesus alone and that He was crucified for us. . . .

"My writing and preaching is nothing else than Jesus Christ. I seek and desire nothing (this the Omniscient One knows) but that the most glorious name, the divine will, and the glory of our beloved Lord Jesus Christ may be acknowledged throughout the world. I desire and seek sincere teachers [ministers], true doctrines, true faith, true sacraments, true worship, and an unblamable life. For this I must pay dearly with so much oppression, discomfort, trouble, labor, sleeplessness, fear, anxiety, care, envy, shame, heat, and cold, and perhaps at last with torture, yes, with my blood and death" (p. 311). Incidentally, this last fear was not realized. Menno died on his sickbed twenty-five years and one day after his renunciation of Catholicism, i.e., on Friday, January 31, 1561.

Ground of hope. "Think not, beloved reader, that we boast of being perfect and without sins. Not at all. . . . By the grace of God I feel, if I but observe the anointing which is in me, when I compare my weak nature to Christ and His commandment, what kind of flesh I have inherited from Adam. . . . Therefore it should be far from us that we should comfort our-

95

selves with anything but the grace of God through Christ Jesus. For He it is and He alone and none other who has perfectly fulfilled the righteousness required by God....

"For Christ's sake we are in grace; for His sake we are heard; and for His sake our faults and failings which are committed against our will are remitted. For it is He who stands between His Father and His imperfect children, with His perfect righteousness, and with His innocent blood and death, and intercedes for all those who believe on Him ..." (p. 506).

Costly discipleship. The sixteenth century was not one of religious toleration. Listen to Menno's complaint: " . . . I with my poor, weak wife and children have for eighteen years [1536-1554] endured excessive anxiety, oppression, affliction, misery, and persecution. At the peril of my life I have been compelled everywhere to drag out an existence in fear. Yes, when the preachers [of the state churches] repose on easy beds and soft pillows, we generally have to hide ourselves in out-of-the-way corners. When they at weddings and baptismal banquets revel with pipe, trumpet, and lute, we have to be on our guard when a dog barks for fear the arresting officer has arrived. When they are greeted as doctors, lords, and teachers [pastors] by everyone, we have to hear that we are Anabaptists, bootleg preachers [unauthorized as ministers by the state], deceivers, and heretics, and be saluted in the devil's name. In short, while they are gloriously rewarded for their services with large incomes and good times, our recompense and portion must be fire, sword, and death" (p. 674).

One of the complicating factors for Menno was the

state of his health. Our only description of him comes from a ferryman named Jan Neulen who took him across a river when he was about fifty years of age. He reported that Menno was a "thick, fat, and heavy man, with a wry facial expression and a brown beard, who had difficulty walking" (Krahn, *Dutch Anabaptism*, p. 184). Menno in his latter years sometimes referred to himself as being crippled (pp. 906n, 919, 1045, 1051, 1056). It appears that he may have suffered a stroke.

What Menno lived for. "I seek neither gold nor silver (the Lord knows) but am ready with faithful Moses to suffer affliction with the people of God rather than to enjoy the pleasures of sin for a season. I also esteem the reproach of Christ greater riches than the treasures in Egypt, for I know what the Scriptures have promised us. This is my only joy and heart's desire; to entend the kingdom of God, reveal the truth, reprove **sin,** teach righteousness, feed hungry souls with the Word of the Lord, lead the straying sheep into the right path, and gain many souls to the Lord through His Spirit, power, and grace. So would I carry on in my weakness as He has taught me who purchased me, a miserable sinner, with His crimson blood, and has given me this mind, by the gospel of His grace, namely Jesus Christ" (p. 189).

V. Effective Ministers

Spirit-empowered. After piling up one figurative description after another of those who serve as ministers in the church, Menno writes: "You see, worthy reader, with such and similar glorious figures and comparisons all pious preachers and teachers are honored in the Scriptures, men whom the Holy Ghost has ordained [as] bishops and overseers in His church. . . . They are motivated by the Spirit of the Lord and urged by unfeigned love. They watch and wait on their assigned duties. They fight courageously every day with the weapon of righteousness. They tear down, break, and destroy all that which is against the Word of God, not by external force with iron and sword, but by the preaching of the holy Word in power and in the Spirit of the Word of the Lord. They till, sow, water, and plant. . . . Their fruits will abide unto eternal life" (pp. 171, 172).

True "teachers" (ministers) "are sent of God, quickened by the Holy Spirit, [they] sincerely seek the salvation of their brethren, who are not earthly minded, but preach the saving, wholesome Word of our beloved Lord Jesus Christ in purity of heart and who are quite unblamable in their doctrine and life" (p. 299). Menno claimed he was not able to find such men in the state churches.

Menno addressed his fellow laborers in the ministry in a book published some two years before his death, beseeching them to see to it "that in all their actions they may so conduct themselves before God and the church, that no man can in truth censure or speak evil of them; as sincere ministers of Christ; faithful and true in all things; men full of the Holy Ghost, born of the incorruptible seed of God . . . transplanted into the good disposition of Christ . . . taught and anointed of God; having their mind on eternal things; averse to their own fame, vainglory, and impure, carnal lusts; humble and small in their own eyes; of a meek and quiet spirit. . . .

"Yes, my brethren, if we could all proceed according to this rule in unity of spirit . . . how soon would the bride of the Lamb shine forth . . . in white and glittering robes . . . (that is, in the beauty of her virtues) . . ." (pp. 995, 996).

Of all Christians it may be said that "Their sword is the sword of the Spirit, which they wield in a good conscience through the Holy Ghost" (p. 94); it is the "the two-edged, powerful sharp sword of the Spirit . . . the Word of God" (p. 424).

Self-employed. We may not feel that Menno's judgment on self-employed ministers is well suited to our age. But Menno thought — perhaps because of his brotherhood concept of the church — that it is advisable for ministers to work, just as do the other members of the church. He does acknowledge that support is rightly given to ministers according to the Word of God, namely, "all the necessities of life" (p. 443). But he seems to think of this as supplementing what the ministers provided for themselves — "which they could not obtain by themselves." Menno insisted that only the church has the right to commission a man to be a preacher. "Wait until you are called of the Lord's church, of the Spirit of God, and are constrained by urging love. . . . Then pastor diligently, preach and teach valiantly, cast from you all filthy lucre and booty; rent a farm, milk cows, learn a trade if possible, do manual labor as did Paul, and all that which you then fall short of will doubtlessly be given and provided you by pious brethren, by the grace of God, not in superfluity, but as necessity requires" (p. 451).

Some insight into Menno's concern is provided in a later book, written to Jelle Smit (Faber), in which

99

Menno declares with feeling: "As long as the world distributes splendid houses and such large incomes to their preachers, the false prophets and deceivers will be there by droves" (p. 663). Menno's final base was New Testament practice: "The true and faithful servants of Jesus in the apostolic churches had nothing to do with such annual stipends, rents, and property, but the greater part earned their bread by their own labor. . . . They have made their own way, and whatever necessities they needed above that they received not of the world [a reference to the state church system], but at the hands of their pious disciples. . . ." (p. 664).

**FOR OTHER FOUNDATION
CAN NO MAN LAY
THAN THAT IS LAID,
WHICH IS JESUS CHRIST** (1 Cor. 8:11).
(Menno's Motto)

7

FILLED
WITH THE
SPIRIT

By Roy S. Koch

I think that I have the most significant topic on the conference program. It looks to me as if everybody and his brother and sister in the Mennonite Church is interested in this topic of the Holy Spirit. Actually, I am excited at what I see happening, at the openness, the hunger, and the interest that there is. I do get around in the church quite a bit and wherever I go, I find people who soon tell me that they have received the baptism of the Holy Spirit and that they speak in tongues and are hungry for the deeper life.

I expected a good attendance at this consultation, but the registration has exceeded my expectations. That, I think, speaks of the great interest there is in this subject of the Holy Spirit and His infilling. This interest is not only in Mennonite circles; it is in other denominations, too, and all around the world. Young people by the thousands are becoming Christians and are filled with the Holy Spirit. They have joined the charismatic movement. It is somewhat like Samuel Shoemaker wrote in 1960. Shoemaker has passed on, but in his book, *With the Holy Spirit and with Fire,* he says,

> What we are feeling for, imagining, longing for, really praying for, is a worldwide awakening unto the power of the Holy Spirit. Maybe it has begun to happen, for there are many signs of the times that are not ominous but hopeful, not filled with foreboding but with promise. Our need for Him and for the awakening which He brings is mounting by the hour. Nothing else on earth seems to me to matter quite so much as that we attempt to put our lives at His disposal so that if He wills to use us, we are there to be used (p. 10).

Of course Samuel Shoemaker knows more about the fullness of the Spirit now since he has passed on, but if he were still living he could now recognize with us that there is a rising tide of new interest in the Holy Spirit all over.

My topic, "Filled with the Spirit," has been walked over and traversed by other speakers in this conference, so maybe I will be repeating some things that have been said before. I shall try not to be too abstract. I should like to be practical, as well as to see what the Bible says about this subject.

The Holy Spirit Filling in the Old Testament

First of all, let us look at some of the examples of Holy Spirit filling in the Old Testament. There is not a great deal on this subject in the Old Testament, but my heart said a great big "Amen" (but quietly like a good Mennonite should), when Brother Myron Augsburger read the passage from Numbers 11, because this is a great passage on the Holy Spirit in the Old Testament. This Scripture tells how the Lord, in an administrative setting, filled seventy people with the Holy Spirit. You well remember that Moses was discouraged. He had a tremendous job on his hands. The people were complaining all the time until Moses could take it no longer. He said, "God, You've got to give me some help. I didn't conceive all these people. Why do You load them on me? I'm not their father."

The Lord said to Moses, "I shall help you. If you designate seventy leaders, I will take the men that you name and will fill them with the Spirit." There is an interesting sidelight about Eldad and Medad in this story. They did not go out to the tabernacle where they were supposed to be for this unique endowment. I have a little pet theory of my own on this point. Maybe I shall do a bit of eisegesis here; eisegesis, you know, is reading something into the Scriptures. I think Eldad and Medad were identical twins. Notice their names. Another guess is that they were under thirty years of age, and still another wild shot is that they were anti-institutional. That is why they did not conform and go out where they should have gone. That's eisegesis, of course.

We have other illustrations from the Old Testament too. Moses was commanded to build a tabernacle. This tabernacle was supposed to be very beautiful indeed, especially on the inside. God said to Moses, "Notice, Moses, that I have called two men, one from the tribe of Dan and one from the tribe of Judah. I have filled them with the Spirit" (not to do preaching or testifying, in this case). "I have filled them with the Spirit because they need to be skilled craftsmen to make all the fine work I want done. I shall give them ability, not only to make the beautiful things I need, but to impart their skills to others as well." This was an infilling of the Spirit to do a particular job.

Of course we all know about Gideon. The Lord told Gideon, "I want you to be the soldier that is going to rid your people of the oppressions of the Midianites." Gideon threw up his hands and said, "Who me? I'm a nobody! I can't take this assignment."

You know the Bible tells us in Judges 6 that the Spirit of the Lord came upon Gideon and transformed this farmer with an inferiority complex into a successful general. In a very real way Gideon became a one-man draft board that raised a competent if not large army almost overnight. Marvel of marvels at what God can do when He fills a person with the Holy Spirit!

Samson is another Old Testament character who was moved by the Spirit of God in a dramatic way. In his case the Spirit endowed him with physical strength. Physically, he had the strength of a giant, but morally and ethically he remained a pygmy. There was one job that God expected him to do and he did it.

The Holy Spirit Filling in the New Testament

I want to illustrate from the New Testament three kinds of Spirit filling. The *first* kind is *the initial filling* of the Holy Spirit. We have looked at the passages

104

that teach this truth a number of times during this convocation. The day of Pentecost is, of course, the greatest example of the filling of the Holy Spirit. Pentecost was the birthday of the church when the Holy Spirit came with great outward demonstration. The apostles, along with the hundred and twenty, were filled with the Holy Spirit and received instant insight. They got courage and were given the gift of tongues so they could praise and magnify God. This was a great experience. Someone has observed that "Pentecost meant the influx of a new power into the life of the disciples for the discharge of a new responsibility." It is true. It was a dramatic change. Those disciples were never the same again after that experience.

There was another Pentecost, a mini-Pentecost if we may call it that, in the house of Cornelius. Peter was summoned to this Gentile's house to explain to him the way of salvation. Those who were with Cornelius were with him in spirit.

Cornelius said, "We want to know how to be saved. An angel told me that you could tell us how to get this experience. I have gathered all my friends and relatives together," he said, "to hear what you have to say."

Peter started preaching. He told about Jesus Christ being baptized with the Holy Spirit and going around in power. Then he followed with the account of Jesus' death and resurrection. I do not know what Peter was planning to do about an invitation, but before he got around to the saving call the whole congregation was converted and started speaking in tongues. What a marvelous surprise! Peter saw the hand of God in this outpouring; so did the rest of his party. It was a never-to-be-forgotten experience.

Paul the apostle, in his travels and preaching, came to Ephesus where he found some people who were Christians, or weren't they? There is some question on this point. They were disciples of John the Baptist who had never heard of the death of Jesus. Paul asked them, "Did you receive the Holy Spirit when you believed?" They said, "We don't know anything about the Holy Spirit." Paul told them, "Your knowledge is deficient. Everything you heard from John the Baptist is true, but there is much more to be had." So he told the full story and baptized them in the name of Jesus Christ. When he followed with the laying on of his hands, they received the Holy Spirit and broke out in praise and in tongues.

In Acts 8 we read that Philip went down to Samaria and conducted a great revival there. Hundreds of people got converted and became joyous in the Lord. But an unusual thing happened at Samaria; these new converts did not receive the Holy Spirit upon believing. How could this be? This is a difficult passage to explain. Peter and John came down from Jerusalem to help the new church members receive what was lacking in their experience. The apostles laid their hands on the Samaritan Christians with the result that they also received the Holy Spirit.

I don't know what sort of demonstrations ensued, but it was evident from their reactions that they received the Holy Spirit. My guess is that they also spoke in tongues, like the apostles did at Pentecost. This is an argument from silence and therefore suspect, but it seems most logical that the proof of their baptism by the Holy Spirit was tongues.

What happened to Saul, the persecuting fanatic, when he was converted in Damascus? Ananias came to him, laid his hands on him, and said, "Brother Saul, the Lord sent me to tell you how to be saved and to be filled with the Holy Spirit." He laid his hands on Saul with the result that Saul's eyes were opened, he was saved, and was filled with the Spirit. Did Saul speak in tongues? There is no record of it, and we would never guess that Saul, or Paul, actually spoke in tongues had he not confessed to it in his epistle to the Corinthians (chap. 14). Even though it is also an argument from silence, how logical to believe that he received this gift when he was baptized by the Holy Spirit upon his conversion.

The incidents referred to before are all illustrations of the initial filling of the Holy Spirit, but there are other dimensions to this filling.

The second kind of Holy Spirit filling is what we call the continuing filling of the Holy Spirit. This teaching is found particularly in Ephesians 5:18. Pardon me for referring to this verse after it has been quoted again and again at this conference. Here Paul tells the Ephesian Christians, "Don't drink too much wine, for many evils lie along that path. Be filled instead with the Holy Spirit and controlled by Him" (*Living Bible*). How should this filling express itself? "Talk with each other much about the Lord, quoting psalms and hymns and singing sacred songs, making music in your hearts to the Lord. Always give thanks for everything to our God and Father in the name of our Lord Jesus Christ."

The passive tense of the Greek verb "to be filled"

suggests that one is receptive to this experience. God is ready to fill you, if you will only be filled. This is to be a constant experience. Charles Inwood comments on this passage as follows:

> There is no such thing as a once-for-all fullness. It is a continuous appropriation of a continuous supply from Jesus Christ Himself. A moment-by-moment faith in a moment-by-moment Savior for a moment-by-moment cleansing and a moment-by-moment filling. As I trust Him, He fills me. So long as I trust Him, He fills me. The moment I begin to believe, that moment I begin to receive. And so long as I keep believing, praise the Lord, so long I keep receiving" (p. 76 in the book, *The Holy Spirit of Promise*, by J. Oswald Sanders).

Isn't that wonderful? In the report from the Presbyterians on the work of the Holy Spirit, which Brother Brunk introduced to us yesterday, I discovered a little quote about this whole matter of the continuing filling of the Holy Spirit.

> The New Testament makes it clear that fullness of the Spirit is an expression referring to the Christian's dependence on the Holy Spirit, a dependence that must be renewed from time to time. Just as forgiveness is to be sought daily, so also a renewed sense of dependence on the enabling power of the Holy Spirit is to be sought for each task to which we put our hands (p. 46, *The Work of the Holy Spirit*).

Is this filling to be an intellectual experience, or is it an emotional experience? I think it is all of them. Shoemaker, who was really on fire for the Lord, said in his book, *With the Holy Spirit and with Fire,*

> The whole appeal of the Holy Spirit is to the total

personality, the mind, the imagination, the will, not the heart only. The experience of the Holy Spirit is made known as a strongly felt presence. Something comes into our energies and capacities and expands them. We are laid hold of by something greater than ourselves (pp. 27, 28).

Of the Corinthian Christians Shoemaker says, as he continues to discuss the Holy Spirit's infilling,

> I doubt if most of them could have given us a coherent account of the Holy Spirit theologically. But they knew Him as an experience. Today we have hundreds of men with trained minds who can tell us all about the Holy Spirit as a third person of the Trinity, but do they know Him as an experience? Today we need not theory but experience, not explanation but living power (p. 34).

I am not sure that I agree entirely with this last statement of Shoemaker's, "We don't need the explanation." I think we do need the explanation. And we have been getting plenty of explanations here at this convocation, but we also need the experience.

In the third place, there are also *bursts of filling for special causes.* Permit me to read about one of these experiences in the Book of Acts. Peter had the initial filling, and I think the continual filling too, but in Acts 4 we are told that Peter is called before the Sanhedrin, the most learned body in Israel. He was really put on the carpet, and it wasn't a red one either. Members of the Sanhedrin said to Peter, "What do you mean by preaching about Jesus?" Acts 4:8 says, "Then Peter, filled with the Holy Spirit, said to them —." In the Spirit-filled speech that Peter gave he confounded these dignitaries. They could not understand Peter's show of courage. "Why," they said, "he is just an ignorant fisherman. How can he talk to us like that?" The answer is, of course, that Peter received a burst of Spirit-filling.

Later in this same chapter, we are told that all the disciples prayed together that the Spirit should manifest Himself to them in boldness. Luke reports the result of that prayer in these words, "The building where they were meeting shook and they were all filled with the Holy Spirit and boldly preached God's message." Here were people who were already Christians and filled with the Spirit, but they experienced an insurge of divine filling. We find this happening again and again in the New Testament.

Sometimes this insurge of the Spirit expressed itself in rather strange and unusual ways. When Paul met unbelieving opposition in the false prophet, Bar-Jesus, he was filled with the Spirit and blazed up in sudden anger and said, "You son of the devil" (*Living Bible*, Acts 13:10). It was a great burst of energy from the Holy Spirit that enabled Paul to meet this challenge to the gospel message.

The Gifts of the Holy Spirit's Infilling

There is another aspect of the Spirit's work in our lives that needs a bit more attention. This is the gifts of the Spirit. Many of you have been giving witness to this dimension of the Spirit's work in your lives. You claim that you have received the baptism of the Spirit subsequent to your conversion. I guess we have a problem here. We know something wonderful has really happened, but we don't have a good name for

110

it. Scholars tell us that this experience is not the baptism of the Spirit, but many of you call it by that name. So what is it? Whatever it is it is often attended with tongues today, as many of you know from personal experience. I want to read a few testimonies about this glorious, deeper work of the Spirit.

A Baptist says, "This river is rising higher than the denominational walls and it is going over them. It's going over every denominational fence and we're swimming together and having this fellowship" (*The New Pentecostalism*, pamphlet).

A Presbyterian said in the same publication, "The gifts of the Spirit began to be distributed among us. We began to see signs, wonders, and miracles, and miracles that have never ceased to this day." *Ibid.*

Another Presbyterian said, "Thousands upon thousands of sane, balanced and cultured people have entered into the experience in this century." *Ibid.*

The 1970 report from the Presbyterians confirms that the experience is real with many people. The report states that some opponents insist that the movement exhibits "a higher level of neuroticism, unadaptive anxiety reactions, a higher degree of susceptibility to suggestion or hysteria, or that charismatic meetings foster such behavior." But the committee that reported their findings rejected these charges with these words, "The data indicate that participants in the movement are emotionally and psychologically quite similar to the normal church population and to their identity group" (p. 12).

E. Stanley Jones in his autobiography, *Song of As-*

cents, reports that when he was a young Christian it seemed to him that his Christian life kept running out. Then he told of a real experience he had with the Lord. The Spirit came upon him with fresh blessing. He said, "All I could do was to walk the floor and praise God. The tears came rolling over my cheeks. Something blessed my soul that hasn't left me to this day." Praise the Lord!

In conclusion, I want to tell you about an incident that happened at the East Goshen Mennonite Church where we attend. Nelson Litwiller conducted renewal meetings for ten days in which he emphasized the work of the Holy Spirit and His liberating power. We had a great heartwarming experience. Last Sunday, the first Sunday after the revival, we had testimonies. A number of people got up and told what God had done for them. One lady said, "Thank God for my healing." She was healed of a physical affliction.

One brother, whose testimony moved us the most, got up and said he had a confession to make. He was one of the leaders of the congregation. He said, "I have my tape recorder in front of me. My wife is in the hospital, and I want her to hear this. That is why I am taping what I am saying."

Then he told about the failures and tensions in his life and relationships. After a while his voice broke. He stood there overcome with emotion, tears were rolling down over his cheeks. I thought he was going to sit down, but he didn't. He stuck right to his guns and insisted on finishing his confession. A great love welled up in my heart for him; I felt like going over to him and embracing him. He wiped his tears, then finished what he wanted to say. Most of the church members were wiping tears. That demonstration of honesty and openness brought the whole congregation together in a real experience of love.

My wife taught a class of young children in the Sunday school period afterward. They wanted to talk about the church service and especially about the brother who wept. He used to have a beard and shaved it off shortly before the meetings began. One of the children made this observation about it, "Maybe he shaved off his beard because he knew he would cry and he didn't want it to get wet." Those of us who are older and really know the Lord know, of course, that there was much more to it than that. But does not such a heartwarming incident demonstrate for us how the Holy Spirit loosens us up, warms our hearts, and brings us all together in a real experience of love?

8

THE ENERGIZING WORK OF THE HOLY SPIRIT

Lessons from the Epistles

By Gerald C. Studer

I. Introduction

The Handbook of Christian Theology (1958) asserts:

The doctrine of the Holy Spirit is . . . the most central . . . doctrine of the Christian faith.[1]

This doctrine enters the realm of theology in terms of an experience rather than that of a concept that can be subjected to the criteria of formal thought. The reality of this experience will always be numinous, i.e., surpassing comprehension, and generally somewhat nebulous. Our Lord implied as much when in John 3:8 He said: "The wind (spirit) blows where it wills, and you hear the sound of it, but you do not know whence it comes or whither it goes; so it is with everyone who is born of the Spirit (wind)." [The parenthesis in both cases is the alternate reading given

114

in a footnote to the RSV. Genesis 1:2 presents a similar illustration in the Old Testament.] But to neglect the Holy Spirit because of ambiguities and difficulties leads the Christian and theology into either intellectualism or a brittle legalism. The Holy Spirit is a divine person and consequently eludes definition and confinement in human terms.

This doctrine is "most central" in the sense that everything reported in the New Testament that is of God is energized and motivated by and through the Holy Spirit's agency. The New Testament, as one commentator has put it, "is preeminently the book of the Holy Spirit." Perhaps this is best dramatized by our Lord Himself when He said that "every sin and blasphemy will be forgiven men . . . (even) whoever says a word against the Son of man . . . but whoever speaks against the Holy Spirit will not be forgiven, either in this age or in the age to come" (Mt. 12:31 f.).

Those who planned this consultation were wise in their choice of words in framing this topic, for some form of the word "energy" has often been used in describing the work of the Holy Spirit. Baker's *Dictionary of Theology* (1960) says:

> The Spirit energizes the body of Christ, the church, to such an extent that her worship (Phil. 3:3; 1 Cor. 14: 15), fellowship (Eph. 4:3; Phil. 2:1), gifts (1 Cor. 12:4-11), and her very origin (1 Cor. 12:13), are due to the animating presence of the Spirit through whom Christ abides in the church."[2]

A Companion to the Bible (1958) observes:

> The Spirit apart from the church would be energy with-

out any instrument through which it could operate. The church without the Spirit would be a body without a principle of life. Therefore in the New Testament the Spirit and the church are always conjoined and are inseparable from each other."[3]

Small wonder then that Christian experience, both individually and collectively, must give attention to the Holy Spirit, for Christianity is as firmly Spirit-centered as it is Christ-centered. For the Spirit is the person of the Trinity by means of which the indwelling and dynamic presence of Christ enables believers to be Christlike and to do His will.

In the New Testament the term "spirit" is accented differently in the Synoptics, in Paul, and in the Johannine writings. I shall not go into its accent in the Gospels since this is not my topic. Neither will I be able to cover the Epistles of James, Peter, John, or Jude. I shall focus on selected passages in the Pauline literature where the place of the Holy Spirit is central. It is indeed the pivotal concept around which all of Paul's specific understandings turn.

More important in Paul's writings than the relation of the Spirit to Jesus' earthly life, is his conception of the Spirit as the mode of Christ's presence in and among His people. In the writings of Luke, the Spirit is, as it were, a line connecting the ascended Christ in heaven with His people on earth. In Paul, on the other hand, the link is more intimate: Christ dwells in the believer and in the Christian community; the believer is "in Christ" and the community is the "body of Christ." The means by which this mutual indwelling takes place is the Holy Spirit, which is the Spirit of Christ Himself.

II. The Teaching of the Pauline Epistles Written Before Paul's Imprisonment

This group includes the Epistles to the Thessalonians (2), Corinthians (2), Galatians, and Romans. Obviously in the time that is allotted to me, I cannot hope to comment on every reference to the Holy Spirit in Paul's letters. Furthermore, I shall admittedly choose those which to me seem most important.

From the very earliest of Paul's Epistles we learn that both in Europe and in Asia Minor the preaching of the gospel was attended by manifestations of the Spirit. In 1 Thess. 1:5 we read: "For our gospel came to you not only in word, but also in power and in the Holy Spirit and with full conviction." This same Spirit which gave strength and assurance to the preachers wrought in the converts such a joyful acceptance of the message that it was not even checked by the violent opposition of the synagogue aided by the aggressively hostile mob.

Nor was it only in this early enthusiasm of their new faith that the Thessalonians manifested the power of the Spirit! In that early Christian world (just as in ours today!) it was a daily struggle for Christians to maintain the purity of life to which God called them. Paul is forthright: "For God has not called us for uncleanness, but in holiness. Therefore whoever disregards this, disregards not man but God, who gives his Holy Spirit to you." This Christian calling moves in a sphere of progressive holiness; Lightfoot paraphrases this last phrase "who is ever renewing this witness against uncleanness in fresh accessions of the Holy Spirit" (4:7, 8).

The Spirit's presence and work was in evidence also in the gift of prophecy. In 5:19-22 Paul admonishes: "Do not quench the Spirit, do not despise prophesying, but test everything; hold fast what is good, abstain from every form of evil." It appears that prophecy was in danger of being undervalued, whether on account of the fact that, as later at Corinth, the more showy gift of tongues was preferred to it, or because it had been abused by some who made wild and even dangerous utterances. But Paul takes a firm stand toward this attitude concerning a great spiritual gift. H. B. Swete paraphrases:

> It is not for believers to throw water on the fire which has been kindled by the Spirit in the heart of a fellow Christian or to make light of utterances which claim to be His inspirations. There is a better course; submit everything of this kind to such tests as may be ready to your hand and as the Spirit itself has given you in the Scriptures, in the experience of life, in the consensus of believers, and retain all that can endure this process. . . .[4]

It is instructive that the second letter presented an instance of such an utterance that had to be rejected as tending toward evil (2 Thess. 2:2). Granted that the above is only one scholar's paraphrase, please note that the test of the prophecy by the Scriptures is not the only test recommended by the apostle.

In reference to his own early ministry at Corinth, the apostle asserts that "my speech and my message were not in plausible words of wisdom, but in demonstration of the Spirit and power" (1 Cor. 2:4). As though to indicate in advance the profound teaching

118

and practical nature of his letters, he said further in
2:12: "Now we have received not the spirit of the
world, but the Spirit which is from God, that we
might understand the *gifts* bestowed on *us* by God."
The italics are mine to emphasize both his intention
to speak to their abuse of a spiritual gift and his
identification with them as the saints he declared them
to be (1:2).

Let us move at once to the passage in these epistles
concerning spiritual gifts. These serve to promote the
enrichment of the Christian life rather than the
ends of personal holiness. We begin with chapters 12
through 14.

The apostle opens with a summary statement:

> "Now there are varieties of gifts,
>   but the same Spirit;
> and there are varieties of service,
>   but the same Lord;
> and there are varieties of working,
>   but it is the same God who inspires them all in
>   every one.
> To each is given the manifestation of the Spirit for the
>   common good."

He then enumerates nine manifestations of the
Spirit. But at this point I ask your permission to veer
from my chronological course of consideration of Paul's
Epistles in order that we might consider at once all
four of the listings Paul gives of the gifts of the
Spirit. We shall attempt this by taking various tacks.
First, let us simply list in order of their appearance
the gifts mentioned in the four places in three
epistles. I shall list them as they are translated by

119

Alfred Marshall in *The Interlinear Greek-English New Testament* (1958).[5]

1 Cor. 12:4-11	*1 Cor. 12:28-31*
word of wisdom	apostles
word of knowledge	prophets
faith	teachers
gifts of cures	powers
operations of powers	gifts of cures
prophecy	helps
discernings of spirits	governings
kinds of tongues	kinds of tongues
interpretation of tongues	

Rom. 12:6-8	*Eph. 4:7-12*
prophecy	apostles
ministry	prophets
teaching	evangelists
exhorting	shepherds/teachers
sharing in simplicity	(teachers)
taking the lead in diligence	
showing mercy in cheerfulness	

Now let us list them in columns, breaking the order in which the individual gifts are listed, but placing those that appear to be identical in the same horizontal line. Where there is uncertainty or difference of opinion, they will be enclosed in brackets with a question mark after them and listed separately also.

	1 Cor. 12:4-11	1 Cor. 12:28-31	Rom. 12:6-8	Eph. 4:7-12
1.	word of wisdom			
2.	word of knowledge			
3.	faith			
4.	gifts of cures	gifts of cures		
5.	operations of powers	powers		
6.	prophecy	prophets	prophecy	prophets
7.	discerning of spirits			
8.	kinds of tongues	kinds of tongues		
9.	interpretation of tongues			
10.			ministry	
11.		teachers	teaching	(teachers?)
12.			exhorting	
13.			sharing in simplicity	
14.			taking lead in diligence	
15.		(helps?)	showing mercy in cheerfulness	
16.		apostles		apostles
17.		governings		
18.				evangelists
19.				shepherds/teachers
20.		helps		

A few observations:

1. If 1 Corinthians is the earliest of the Pauline Epistles containing such lists, the first of the two lists is also the longest of all four, the others decreasing in number of gifts mentioned as the letters are written later in time.

2. The only gift listed in all four groups is that of *prophecy* or *prophets*. Is there a better way to determine the relative importance of the gifts — if indeed Paul had any intention to listing them in an order of importance? Only one, and one of these doubtful, is listed three times. Four are listed twice each, with a possibility of one additional.

3. There appears to be little ground for speaking of any specific number of spiritual gifts — it rather looks as though the apostle had nothing more in mind than to illustrate what he was saying in the larger context, and this suggested various-sized and somewhat random groups of examples.

4. Dr. Klaas Runia in a recent *Eternity* magazine article on "The Third Work of the Spirit" says:

> The New Testament repeatedly speaks of the wonderful gifts of the Spirit. . . . Several times we find spectacular gifts such as speaking in tongues and healing. But the less spectacular are even more prominent. These include . . . prophecy, evangelism, service (e.g., Dorcas — Acts 9:36), and administration (e.g., deacons in Acts 6).[6]

He mentions also that Peter writes about the Spirit's gifts in 1 Peter 4:8-11. These are somewhat indistinct though possibly hospitality, speaking, and ministry are mentioned. See also 1 Cor. 14:6.

5. What is the difference between the utterance of wisdom and that of knowledge? Runia comments that even Pentecostals who claim to possess these gifts explain them differently.

6. The principal purpose of all the gifts is the edification and unity of the church. (Rom. 12:4 ff.; 1 Cor. 12:12 ff.; Eph. 4:4 ff.) Even those designed more for personal edification such as tongues have some value to the corporate body — see 1 Cor. 14:22. Yet the variety is also emphasized (Rom. 12:6; 1 Cor. 12:4 ff.; Eph. 4:7) but the unity is first and fundamental and the variety second and subsequent.

7. Imperfections or abuses in the exercise of the gifts do not mean that the gifts are either not genuine or that they are dispensable. Genuine gifts can be wrongly used because of the imperfections of the believer. Also, it must be remembered that the possession of a gift does not make the believer perfect or superior to other believers.

First Corinthians 12:29 emphasizes that the less dramatic gifts and functions are not less necessary to the life and work of the whole organism than those more "showy" ones. It is further suggested that their absence or depreciation destroys the completeness, the balance, and even the efficiency of the body of Christ. All are in their degree manifestations of the presence of the divine Spirit of which all believers are partakers. The argument Paul uses with such cogency in 12:14-25 is indeed to the correction of the very abuses to which Paul proceeds to address himself with such candidness and force.

Ellicott gives quite a different turn to verses 29, 30 than that given by so many evangelicals and I am inclined to believe that it is the better understanding of Paul's line of thought. He believes a better translation is "but earnestly seek the better gifts." Then he says:

> All this argument is not meant to check ardor and to damp enthusiasm. The Spirit divideth to every man as He wills, but He wills to give to each the best gift that each desires and is capable of receiving. The receptivity which comes with earnest and practical desire is in the case of each individual the determining cause as to what gift the Spirit will give. The last sentence, "And yet shew I unto you a more excellent way," ought to form the opening clause of the next chapter. The "more excellent way" is *not* some gift to be desired to the exclusion of the other gifts *but a more excellent way of striving for those gifts*. You are not to strive for any one gift because it is more highly esteemed, or because it is more apparently useful, or because it is more easily attained. That which will consecrate every struggle for attainment and every gift when attained is LOVE.[7] (Italics mine)

I cannot accept Swete's interpretation that there is in the first Corinthian list of the gifts a certain order and that they are "in the orderly sequence of a descending scale," for if prophecy is indeed one of the so-called higher gifts and is therefore mentioned in all four lists, then it is strange that Paul should in 1 Corinthians 13 so quickly demean it by mentioning in quick succession tongues, prophecy, and sharing one's goods (knowledge is also mentioned later), as being profitless if exercised without love. True, all of the gifts will ultimately be "done away," but it is interesting to note that Paul seems to have no in-
124

terest in favoring any of the gifts above another when pointing out the necessity of their being exercised in the proper context and motive and in love.

While love is to be the preeminent object of our acts, thoughts, and attitudes, yet Paul proceeds to say, "Pursue love, but desire eagerly the spiritual gifts, and rather in order that you may prophesy." Paul reminds his readers that the prophet could "build up" the church by exhorting and consoling its members, and even winning unbelievers who entered its assemblies. Nevertheless, the apostle does not forbid tongues or allow prophecy to run riot uncontrolled. Both were gifts of the Spirit and each has its place, but both must be exercised under proper restraints.

Even though prophecy may have a superior place in Paul's mind for corporate worship, he reminds them that prophets' spirits are under prophets' control, so that the prophet is responsible for the use of his gift. If he abuses his gift or if he is a mere pretender or is under influences which are not of the Spirit of God, there is another gift, the discerning of spirits, by which he can and ought to be called to account. Swete says: "A free criticism of prophetic utterances by men who were qualified by the possession of the critical spirit is not only permitted but encouraged."[8] 1 Cor. 14:29.

To continue our chronological survey of the Epistles of Paul, in Galatians the work of the Spirit first comes into view in chapter 3: "Let me ask you only this: Did you receive the Spirit by works of the Law, or by hearing with faith? . . . Having begun with the Spirit, are you now ending with the flesh? . . .

125

Does he who supplies the Spirit to you and works miracles among you do so by works of the law, or by hearing with faith?" (vv. 2, 3, 5). Paul resorts to sarcasm in expressing his keen disappointment at their possible entry on the downgrade road of external rites. Notice the reminder that it is God who continually supplies the Spirit and makes possible those powers among them (cf. 1 Cor. 12:10, 28). Had the law-keeping party anything of this kind to show?

Further the apostle is led by his line of thought to speak of the Spirit as the Spirit of the Son. The Spirit of the only begotten Son is sent into the hearts of the adopted sons, because He is the very Spirit of sonship. This Spirit does not make them sons, for they are such by virtue of their rebirth, but rather makes them conscious of their sonship and capable of fulfilling their responsibilities and privileges. "Without the mission of the Spirit, the mission of the Son would have been fruitless; without the mission of the Son, the Spirit could not have been sent."[9]

A group of passages follows in Galatians in which the contrast between Spirit and flesh is elaborated upon. We shall proceed directly to that statement of radical antagonism between flesh and Spirit which Paul makes in 5:16, 17. Paul names a dreary and disgusting brood of offspring of the flesh followed by a roll-call of the fruit of the Spirit, reminding his law-and-order readers that law can neither produce nor forbid such beautiful and necessary qualities as these.

Romans opens with a reference to an antithesis — according to the flesh/according to the Spirit of holiness — but here it is in reference to the incarnation and resurrection and not to the radical antagonism that he set up in his Galatian letter. However, the sharp contrast between Spirit and law/flesh emerges in this Epistle also (see chapter 7). He admits to a serious schizophrenia within man apart from Christ. "But ye are not in flesh but in Spirit since the Spirit of God dwells in you" (8:9).[10] And it is this indwelling of the Spirit which Paul pauses to remind his readers lays the believer under an obligation to live as the Spirit directs. (8:12 ff.) To fail to pay this obligation in life, thought, and word day by day is to quench and to grieve the Spirit, if not eventually to expel Him from your life. The Spirit's presence and practical sovereignty in our hearts will produce an inner sense of peace and security and will expel all spirit of slavery and fear. (8:14-17.) The experience of suffering in this life does not cast a doubt upon our sonship but is rather on the direct road to realizing the glory of the children of God. The apostle reminds us that in this life *our* emancipation, along with that of all creation, is incomplete and awaits the redemption of our body. (8:23.)

This brings us to a truth of which Swete says:

> There is perhaps nothing in the whole range of New Testament Pneumatology which carries us so far into the heart of the Spirit's work.[11]

Paul has spoken of the groans of suffering Nature being shared by the half-emancipated children of God. Meanwhile, he says, we are not left without effective help in our struggle with sin and death. The very Spirit of God within us bears His part in our present difficulties. As He cries in us and we in Him, "Abba, Father," so He shares the groans of

127

our imperfect nature, converting them into prayers without and beyond words. Swete says it well:

> There are times when we cannot pray in words, or pray as we ought; but our inarticulate longings for a better life are the Spirit's intercessions on our behalf, audible to God who searches all hearts, and intelligible and acceptable to Him since they are the voice of His Spirit, and it is according to His will that the Spirit should intercede for the members of His Son. . . . The mystery of prayer stands here revealed, as far as it can be in this life; we see that it is the Holy Spirit who not only inspires the filial spirit which is the necessary condition of prayer, but is the author of the very "hearty desires" which are its essence.[12]

Paul in his closing words admonishes the Roman Christians to be "fervent in spirit" thus reflecting the same hatred of lukewarmness that our Lord expressed in Revelation 3:16. Paul later urged Timothy to rekindle his zeal (2 Tim. 1:6). Paul freely acknowledges at the end of his missionary journeys that all he had accomplished had been wrought by Christ through his hands in the power of the Spirit (15:18 f.).

III. The Teaching of the Pauline Epistles Written During or After Paul's Imprisonment

This group includes Philippians, Colossians, Ephesians, First and Second Timothy, and Titus. Even though it is doubtful that Paul had any idea that his letters would comprise about 1/4 of the Christian Scriptures and would be diligently read and studied nearly 2000 years later, it seems characteristic of him that he does not return, except incidentally or for a practical purpose, to a subject

128

which he has treated at some length in an earlier Epistle. It may well have been that the needs of various persons and congregations to which he wrote were just that different! Today also every Christian church has a unique "personality." At any rate, the doctrine of the Holy Spirit does not again come up for discussion in this later group of Epistles.

However, the work of the Holy Spirit enters so largely into the life of the church, and held so prominent a place in the thought of the apostolic age, that no New Testament letter (except Philemon) to the churches or even to an individual could fail altogether to mention the Spirit.

Philippians 1:19 expresses an amazing truth in that Paul declares confidently that even the preaching of the gospel on the part of some in a spirit of partisanship and in the hope of adding affliction to his bonds, will turn out to be to his salvation "through your petition and supply of the Spirit of Jesus Christ" (Phil. 1:19). The prayers of the Philippian church and the supply of the Spirit to the apostle in his imprisonment at Rome are so closely related that in the Greek one article suffices for the two. Paul had written similarly several years earlier of the Spirit as "supplied" through the ministry of the Galatian church (Gal. 3:5). So vitally does our Lord tie us not only to Himself but also to our fellow believers that the exercise of the diverse gifts is to be subservient to the love and unity that are to prevail throughout the body. This concern for the unity of the body at Philippi is evident in verses 27 through 2:3. One commentator holds that "fellowship of the Spirit" (2:1) "is more than oneness of

129

spirit; it is that joint participation in the Spirit's gifts and powers which was in the apostolic church the acknowledged bond of unity and communion between the baptized."[13]

There is only the most passing reference to the Spirit in Colossians (1:8). But Ephesians abounds in references to the Holy Spirit, and in some of these, new facets of the Spirit's work are indicated.

It is significant to associate Ephesians 4:30 with 1: 13, 14, since two keys words occur in both. Believers received the *seal* of the Spirit with a view to their complete *redemption* at a future day. This thought of a "day of redemption" adds another motive to that which the apostle appeals to in his argument against the indulgence of sin in 1 Thess. 4:8, for this reference places the present struggle against sin in the light of the day of Christ. Consequently the apostle exhorts against grieving the Spirit since to have received the seal of the Spirit is not only a cause for thankfulness but a source of increased responsibility. The first installment (earnest) of spiritual life which the Spirit brings is not an absolute guarantee of ultimate salvation; it points to that end but may be frustrated by the conduct of the person who has received it. In effect the apostle is saying: "You were sealed with the Spirit . . . then do not break the seal."

At this point I am faced with a difficult problem. My allotted time must be up and I have but scarcely begun to speak of the materials concerning the Holy Spirit in Ephesians, not to mention the two Epistles to Timothy and one to Titus. I shall try to close with only the briefest comments.

I doubt that Paul has in mind the charismatic "word of wisdom" when he breaks into a prayer (1:17 ff.) for the believers at Ephesus. It would seem rather to be an expression of his deep desire that all believers may have such a vigorously growing knowledge of Christ that they never cease to be both intrigued and amazed at His grace and power toward them. In 2:14 he sees a new humanity in the union of Jew and Gentile in the body of Christ. In chapter 4 the apostle enumerates seven unities which are to triumph over all the elements of discord that tend to divide believers. In this same chapter Christ's gifts are connected with the ascension, and their purpose is to perfect the church of Christ. In 5:18 f. we find Paul boldly contrasting the exhilarating power of the Spirit with the effect of an excess of wine. It is not the use of wine that is deprecated but its abuse. Christians need not feel cheated when expected to abstain from the shallow mirth produced by the stimulation of wine, for they are to know a compensation that is a deeply permanent stimulation and for this there is all manner of music by which they might give vent to their joy. Finally, life in Christ is also a warfare with the powers of evil and for this the Spirit supplies Christians with their chief weapon of attack and defense, namely, God's Word (6:17).

In 1 Timothy 4:1 we very probably have a Christian prophecy cited. Later in the same chapter, Timothy is reminded of the prophecy that likely marked him out as the future companion of Paul and led to his ordination. It may well have been a scene much like that recorded in Acts 13 where a word from the Holy Spirit through the prophets and teachers gathered in worship designated Barnabas and Saul for the work to which the Spirit was calling them. Second Timothy 1 then alludes to the ordination of Timothy and calls him to stir up the gift which was given by Paul's laying-on-of-hands. Timothy was possibly recoiling from the bold witness to Christ and the consequent afflictions to which he was called (2 Tim. 1:6-9).

IV. Summary

Let me attempt to summarize in a series of brief statements the main points I have attempted to make:

1. We must not neglect the Holy Spirit simply because He transcends definition. The New Testament is preeminently both the fruit and an account of the Holy Spirit's energizing work.

2. The Holy Spirit is the person of the Trinity through which the indwelling and dynamic presence of Christ provides power within both the Christian and the church.

3. The preaching of the gospel may be expected to produce manifestations of the Spirit, such as conviction of sin and both the fruit and gifts of the Spirit.

4. The Holy Spirit instructs us to test all manifestations to see whether they are in accord with the words and principles of Christ.

5. Believers are to guard against quenching and grieving the Spirit in His work.

6. It is doubtful that Paul intends to place the gifts of the Spirit in any order of importance; it seems rather that he desires to emphasize that their exercise must be in Christian love and in harmony with the unity of the Spirit.

7. The principal purpose of the Spirit's ministry in and among believers is the edification and unity of the church.

8. The work of the Spirit among believers is forfeited by any reversion to the keeping of law.

9. There is a radical antagonism between the Spirit and the flesh in Christian experience. Our emancipation from sin and death will be incomplete in this life, but our living "in the Spirit" makes possible a life of fruit-bearing, freedom from guilt, and a deep joy.

10. The Spirit intercedes for us at all times and with sighs too deep for words.

11. Having the seal of the Spirit places upon the Christian an increased responsibility to be faithful to Christ and His Word.

12. The apostle earnestly warns against lukewarmness and admonishes us to "never flag in zeal, (but rather) be aglow with the Spirit!" (Rom. 12:11, parenthesis mine).

V. *Conclusion*

From beginning to end, whether in references to our personal Christian lives or the life of the church, the profound and unmistakable fact is that every inch of progress toward the accomplishment of that ultimate will of God is both inspired, empowered, and accomplished in and through us by the energizing work of the Holy Spirit.

I can scarcely imagine a more exalted and appropriate conclusion to this examination of St. Paul's teaching on the person and work of the Holy Spirit than is found in the words of his prayer found in Ephesians 1:16 when he says his prayer is:

"that the God of our Lord Jesus Christ, the Father of glory,

may give you a spirit of wisdom and of revelation in
the knowledge of him,
having the eyes of your hearts enlightened,
that you may know what is the hope to which he has
called you,
what are the riches of his glorious inheritance in the
saints,
and what is *the immeasurable greatness of his power
in us who believe*
according to the working of his great might which he
accomplished in Christ
when he raised him from the dead and made him sit
at his right hand
in the heavenly places, far above all rule and
authority and power
and dominion, and above every name that is named,
not only in this
age but also in that which is to come,
and he has put all things under his feet
and has made him the head over all things for the
church,
which is his body, the fullness of him who fills all
in all."

(Italics mine)

Footnotes

Footnotes: (Unless otherwise noted, all quotations from Scripture are in the
Revised Standard Version.)
1. *Handbook of Christian Theology* (New York: Living Age Books, 1958). p.
170.
2. Everett F. Harrison, *Baker's Dictionary of Theology* (Grand Rapids:
Baker Book House, 1960). p. 496.
3. J. J. Von Allmen, *A Companion to the Bible* (New York: Oxford, 1958).
p. 171.
4. Henry Barclay Swete, *The Holy Spirit in the New Testament* (London:
Macmillan & Co., 1921). p. 173.

5. Alfred Marshall, *The Interlinear Greek-English New Testament* (London: Samuel Bagster & Sons, 1958).
6. *Eternity,* January 1972, "The Third Work of the Spirit" by Klaas Runia, p. 19.
7. *Ellicott's New Testament Commentary,* Vol. VII (London: Cassell & Company, Ltd., n.d.). p. 122.
8. Swete, *op. cit.,* p. 189.
9. *Ibid.,* p. 206.
10. Marshall, *op. cit.*
11. Swete, *op. cit.,* p. 221.
12. *Ibid.,* p. 221.
13. *Ibid.,* p. 229.

9

THE
PROPHETIC WORK
OF THE
SPIRIT

Lessons from Revelation 2 and 3

By J. Otis Yoder

Introduction

We have been informed by the scholars of the Scripture and by the students of prophecy, in particular, that the word "prophecy" has a twofold meaning. It means first, prediction of the future. That may be for a period of a day, a year, or hundreds of years, or even millenniums. Second, it means admonishing and instruction of the hearers regarding the times. And just to reduce these meanings to very simple language we have been told that a prophet may be on the one hand a foreteller and on the other hand a forthteller. What has happened to our study of the prophetic word is that we have overstressed the forthtelling at the expense of the foretelling.

Indeed it was Carl F. H. Henry at the Jerusalem Conference on Biblical Prophecy in June, 1971, who said, "We have so stressed the forthtelling of the prophets that their foretelling has little meaning for us today." I believe we should take special note of Carl F. H. Henry's analysis of our trends.

It is certainly true that many of the prophets, both Old and New Testament, spoke beyond their times to times yet to come. This we should never lose sight of, even though we may be analyzing a given prophetic passage for its practical and timeless lessons.

In the fall of 1961 while studying in the city of Jerusalem, Pierre Faye-Hansen, a Scandinavian pastor from Haifa, was lecturing at the American Institute of Holy Land Studies. The subject of his series of lectures was "Israel in Prophecy." During his opening lecture he made a profound statement. He said, "Eschatology cannot be on the perimeter of your theology. It must be at the heart of your theology." We believe that Mr. Hansen was right. Without the sense of destiny and end, our theology is of little worth. We may even go a bit farther and say that history without an eschatology equals nonsense, for the Bible makes clear from one cover to the other that the God who began human history is going to finish it. Without the fact of the divine purpose in human history the present has no meaning and no cohesiveness. This may be the reason why in recent years we have found so many people who feel life isn't worth it anymore. Without there being an end there can be no purpose now.

Since history and theology both must have an end we cannot ignore the predictive aspect of the prophetic ministry of the Holy Spirit. And indeed Jesus old the disciples, "I have yet many things to say unto you, but ye cannot bear them now; nevertheless when he, the Spirit of truth, is come, he will guide you into all truth, for he shall not speak of himself, but whatsoever he shall hear, that shall he speak and he will show you things to come" (Jn. 16:12, 13). We must, therefore, conclude without question, that part of the ministry of the Holy Spirit was to reveal new truths to the disciples, or we may say, to add to the body of truth already revealed. It is of particular significance to bear in mind that in the body of revealed truth there are great lobes of predictive prophecy. These, I say, we cannot ignore.

To turn more directly to the book under discussion for this topic, for I note we are to draw lessons from Revelation 2 and 3, a few comments will be in order regarding this last book of the Holy Scriptures. Let us pay particular attention to the name of the book. It is said to be "a Revelation of Jesus Christ, which God gave unto him, to shew unto his servants things which must shortly come to pass; and he sent and signified it by his angel unto his servant, John, who bare witness of the word of God, and of the testimony of Jesus Christ, and of all things that he saw" (Rev. 1: 1, 2). It is commonly conceded that the word "revelation" means "unveiling." It means to draw aside the curtain. It means to bring forth new truth or the expansion of old truth; to push back the horizons of understanding. We accept this as a valid definition for the Book of Revelation. Consequently, we must be prepared for unusual insights and further exploration of divine truth.

It is easily and early discernible that the Book of Revelation is not an epistle parallel to the epistles of Paul. That is to say, it is of a different nature and character. It is so because the writer of the Book of Revelation makes larger claims than any other New Testament writer, for the source materials of his book. Nowhere do we find in Paul's letters that he wrote with the same sense of direct communication with heaven. Observe again that Revelation 1:1 states it precisely that what John wrote in this book was received directly from Jesus Christ through the informing angel. His claim to the material in hand is direct and immediate.

In the full context of this book the Apostle John asserts 44 visions and 28 auditions. No other book in all of Holy Writ has this same claim to direct and immediate revelation. Thus the Book of Revelation must be taken for what it is — an unveiling of events, conditions, and scenes before to man unknown and unknowable. We may further point this up by careful examination of chapter 1:10. "I was in the Spirit on the Lord's day, and heard behind me a great voice, as of a trumpet. . . ." Here is the crux of our interpretative processes. How we understand this verse will determine how we understand the rest of the Book of Revelation.

A careful translation of the words immediately above will give us this understanding: "I came to be in the Spirit in the day of the Lord, and heard behind me a great voice, as of a trumpet. . . ." At once we catch the significance of the prophetic ministry of the Spirit in the composition of this Book of Revelation. The Apostle John was in the tradition of the great prophets of the Old Testament. Indeed Ezekiel was lifted up by the Spirit of God and transported to the city of Jerusalem, on one occasion, and into the valley of dry bones on another occasion, Ezekiel 37. We should not be surprised then, if another of the prophets of God, John on the island of Patmos, would experience a similar transportation. Thus, the Holy Spirit functioned in the life of the beloved disciple to bring before him conditions, events, and scenes before unknown and indeed unknowable to man.

The phrase usually translated in English versions, "on the Lord's day," has been amply explained and its proper interpretation set forth in the J. B. Smith commentary on the Book of Revelation entitled, *A Revelation of Jesus Christ,* Herald Press, pages 319 to 324. We must, therefore, not shortchange our understanding of this great book nor of these two chapters under consideration in this message by limiting the action of the Spirit to Sunday.

A second consideration that must be examined is the identification of the voice which the Apostle John heard. As he turned to see the voice we have him describing a scene never before witnessed by man. He saw One, he said, like the Son of man. The description which he gives is both awful and awesome. He who walked among men as the humblest of men, appeared to the Apostle John with such awe-inspiring dignity and reality that he says, "And when I saw him, I fell at his feet as dead" (Rev. 1:17). The difference is so marked and the description is such a contrast that we must not lose sight of it. When He came the first time, He came as a suffering Savior. None fell at His feet as dead then, excepting the demon-possessed. They knew Him and always acknowledged His sovereignty. But, in this experience, Jesus' beloved disciple fell at His feet as dead. Now He is Lord of lords in all His awful and awesome reality.

As one examines the various descriptions that the Apostle John gave of Him, it is not difficult to see that He has the right to examine the life of the church and certainly the life of each individual believer.

Let us note further that the position of Him who is so described was in the midst of the seven churches. The seven golden lampstands which the seer saw first are described as the seven churches and we may observe quickly that He was in the midst of the seven lampstands. He had, furthermore, seven stars in His right hand. The seven stars are interpreted as the angels of the seven churches. We cannot mistake, then, that the Lord of lords in all His awesome and awful reality stands in the midst of the churches and has the right to make His investigations and pronounce His approbations and condemnations, as the case may be.

Let us note the following analysis which J. B. Smith give in his *A Revelation of Jesus Christ* (Herald Press) pp. 53, 54 in "Attributes of the Son of Man as Suggested by the Symbolism in Verses 13-16."

1. In the midst of the seven candlesticks: love and familiarity.
2. Clothed with a garment down to the foot: righteousness and dignity.
3. Girt about the paps with a golden girdle: compassion and virility.
4. His head and his hairs . . . white like wool, as white as snow: eternity and wisdom.
5. His eyes . . . as a flame of fire: omniscience and scrutiny.
6. His feet like unto fine brass, as if they burned in a

141

furnace: judgment and purity.

7. His voice as the sound of many waters: grandeur and dignity.
8. And he had in his right hand seven stars: omnipotence and authority.
9. Out of his mouth went a sharp twoedged sword: truth and severity.
10. His countenance . . . as the sun shineth in his strength: holiness and glory.

Let us make a few more observations before entering into chapters 2 and 3 for our lessons. The seer was told that he was to write what he saw in a book and "send it to the seven churches which are in Asia, unto Ephesus and unto Smyrna and unto Pergamos and unto Thyatira and unto Sardis and unto Philadelphia and unto Laodicea." We should remember that these seven churches were located in Asia Minor. William Ramsay suggests that the churches chosen were the centers of evangelistic efforts in their territories and thus they are representative of larger areas where proclamation of the gospel was being carried on. He also suggests that these seven churches were in the seven cities connected by one of the main trade routes of the area. Thus it became a simple matter for a post to carry the letter or book from one to the other.

As one takes his position on the Island of Patmos and looks over to the continent of Asia Minor, it immediately becomes evident that the seven churches form an inverted "V" beginning with Ephesus and ending with Laodicea. We may raise the question, Why would Jesus have chosen these seven churches in Asia

Minor? For there were more churches in Asia Minor than these seven. The Acts of the Apostles states clearly that the Apostle Paul carried on gospel work in much of the area and had planted churches in various parts of the provinces of Asia Minor. Perhaps the question cannot be satisfactorily answered for all of us. Some would say that the choice of these seven churches was deliberately made by the Lord Jesus and that He was seeing in them the several epochs of church history mirrored from the apostolic era to the end. This is somewhat intriguing as one follows through the various analyses of the churches. Others would say that the selection of these seven churches was simply made because they were representing the universal and timeless church and that one can expect to find the conditions outlined in these seven churches at any period in church history.

Now it is not our purpose to debate these points of view. It is rather to point out that these were seven historical churches and that the Lord chose them as recipients of this book for a particular reason which we may not have disclosed to us. And yet, at the same time, it is not without significance that one can trace the various analyses and see a rather clear pattern emerging.

We may, therefore, come now to the question which is immediately before us. What lessons can we learn from these messages to the seven churches, Revelation 2 and 3?

May I suggest to you that among the many lessons we may learn there are four outstanding lessons that we cannot overlook, if we are to understand the prophetic word of the Spirit.

I. The Son and the Spirit Cooperate

It was called to our attention in the introduction that the Apostle John was in the Spirit in the day of the Lord and he heard the Son of man speaking to him. When one opens the second chapter of Revelation he discovers that the One who stands in the midst of the seven lampstands is going to address the church at Ephesus. He had exactly the position that the Apostle John saw Him have, when he first turned to see. He's there to present His case, to offer His analyses of conditions of the church.

It is also significant that at the end of the message to Ephesus the word comes through, "He that hath an ear, let him hear what the Spirit saith unto the churches." Do you see in this the cooperation of the penetrating and probing Christ with the arresting Holy Spirit? This pattern one finds throughout all seven letters. But note, to the church at Smyrna, it is the One who was dead and is alive. The implication of His crucifixion and resurrection is clearly there. But again the arresting word comes, "He that hath an ear, let him hear what the Spirit saith unto the churches."

It should also be clear, turning to the letter to the church at Pergamos, where the penetrating, probing Christ is described as the One who has a sharp sword with two edges. This truth carries with it the threat that Jesus would fight with the sword of His mouth against those who do not repent. Here again the word, "He that hath an ear, let him hear what the Spirit saith unto the churches." It should be observed before going on that here is a distinct unity of the Son and the Word and the Spirit. That comes quickly to the surface in the church in Pergamos.

Moving on to the church at Thyatira, the probing, penetrating Christ is shown as One whose eyes are as a flame of fire and His feet like fine brass. But again, "He that hath an ear, let him hear what the Spirit saith unto the churches." It should be noted that a shift in location of this arresting word has taken place. The messages to the first three churches, the overcomer's promise came last. Now the arresting word of the Spirit comes last and it is so from here on.

We observe from the church at Sardis that he who hath the seven spirits and seven stars is He who comes to speak. But once more, "He that hath an ear, let him hear what the Spirit saith unto the churches."

With Philadelphia, it is He who is holy and true, who has the key of David, who presents Himself to the church. Once more, let him hear what the Spirit saith. And finally to the church of the Laodiceans it is the "Amen, the faithful and true witness, the beginning of the creation of God" who brings His message. But again, the arresting word, "He that hath an ear, let him hear what the Spirit saith unto the churches."

Note the various descriptions of the One who stands in the midst of the churches, from Him who is in the midst of the seven lampstands: to Him who is alive, though He was dead, to Him who has the sharp sword, to Him who has the eyes as a flame of fire, to Him to whom belong the seven spirits of God, to Him who is true and has the key of David, and to Him who is the amen, the faithful and true witness. To all of these, there comes the resounding word, "He that hath an ear, let him hear what the Spirit saith unto the churches."

It should be clear then that God is not divided. The Son and the Spirit cooperate in the analyses of the churches, in the messages to these seven churches. Someone has very well said, you can be a unitarian in one of three ways. You can overemphasize the work of the Father at the expense of the Son and the Spirit. You can overemphasize the work of the Son at the expense of the Father and the Spirit. You can overemphasize the work of the Spirit at the expense of the Father and the Son. You can be a unitarian in one of three ways.

One lesson we can learn from the message to the seven churches is that God is not divided. The Son and the Spirit and the Word cooperate.

II. *The Son and the Spirit Penetrate*

We may go farther now to our second lesson and come back to these letters again to observe what the penetrating Christ has to say about these churches, each of them a local assembly. Each of them, perhaps, representing a universal situation. Each of them, perhaps, representing a certain era.

There are two phrases that must catch our attention as we draw this lesson.

1. *I know.* You will observe as you glance down over these letters that this comes early in the presentation of truth. What does this say to us? This tells us, I assert, that nothing is hidden from the Lord of the church. The church is His body. He knows what is going on in the church. You will note that almost without exception the penetrating Christ says, "I know thy works." I know what you are going through. I

146

know what you are tolerating. I know what you are against. I know how weak-spined you are.

Notice, to the church at Ephesus He says, "I know thy works, and thy labour, and thy patience, and how thou canst not bear them which are evil: and thou hast tried them which say they are apostles, and are not, and hast found them liars: and hast borne, and hast patience, and for my name's sake hast laboured, and hast not fainted." Now in each of the letters, we see this same kind of underneath-the-surface probing and penetrating and finding the actual situation in each one of the churches. Note, however, that with the church at Smyrna, the church at Sardis, and the church at Laodicea the analysis which the Lord makes is quite different from what the superficial judge might make. To Smyrna He said, "I know thy poverty, (but thou art rich)." To the church in Sardis He said, "I know thou hast a name that thou livest, and art dead." To the church in Laodicea, He said, "Because thou sayest, I am rich, but you don't know that you are wretched, and miserable, and poor, and blind, and naked."

The Son and the Spirit penetrate beneath the surface. They are able to see the real conditions of each local assembly. *I know* carries with it tremendous implications which cannot be set aside. We stand under the penetrating gaze of the Lord of the church.

2. *I have.* The second phrase that must be caught again is only two words, *I have.* In five of the seven churches, the message of the penetrating Son and Spirit is simply, "I have somewhat against thee," or, "I have a few things against thee." Note carefully what those few things are.

In the case of Ephesus, it was the leaving of their first love which was a score against them. All of their other activities could not outweigh the fact that they had left their first love. They were urged to remember their first love and to do the first works. It is not difficult to see what pain this would bring to the Master, the Lord of the church.

To Smyrna, the Lord did not say, "I have somewhat against thee." He did say, however, that He understood the perversions that were attempted. He saw through the hypocrisy of those who claimed to be Jews and are not. The significance of this statement may not be altogether clear to us, but it has some very deep undercurrents. Are there not some today who claim to be Jews and are not? At least they would attempt to steal the promises from the Jews, it would seem.

To the church at Pergamos, the Lord said, "I have a few things against thee." We might note that here the Lord was greatly distressed over the fact that the church had lost her sense of distinctiveness by drawing the analogy from Balak and Balaam. Israel lost her sense of distinctiveness, too, and went to the idol altars and to sacrifice unto idols and to commit fornication. Has not the church today lost her sense of distinctiveness? Nonconformity, which was once a precious doctrine, has become ridiculed and set on the shelf with other artifacts of ancient times. But does not the Spirit, does not the penetrating Son and Spirit, call to our attention today that we cannot find our satisfaction at the altar of idols without the high price with which He threatened the church at Pergamos?

To the church at Thyatira the Lord said, "I have a few things against thee." It may be very clearly and quickly reduced to this. The church at Thyatira permitted false doctrine to be taught and disseminated among them. Jezebel taught and seduced God's servants to commit fornication and to eat things sacrificed to idols. Fornication in its spiritual setting has always meant to go against known truth. The penetrating Son and Spirit, I believe, would need to come to us in our day and would say, "I have a few things against thee." False teaching has a way of permeating the meal of truth until it is all leavened.

To the church at Sardis He said, "I have somewhat against thee," not with these precise words, but with the words, "I have not found thy works perfect before God." We may conclude, just by a quick reading, that the church at Sardis was guilty of flexibility, of indolence, they lacked vigilance, they were not on guard. They felt smugly content. Jesus said, I am not satisfied with that. Historically we are told that the city of Sardis fell because the defenders were not alert. It may be that Jesus is using this as an illustration, though slightly veiled, to call attention to the fact that destruction can come when people are engaged in other matters. The church at Sardis was guilty of flexibility.

Again to the church at Philadelphia the Lord does not say, "I have somewhat against you." However, let me point out to you that in a veiled way He does say, I have certain corrections to make. Like the church at Smyrna, there were those who moved among the Philadelphians under guise of being Jews and were not really. Let us not lose the importance of this.

It is implied, it would seem, that those who paraded under this type of hypocrisy would be exposed and they would find themselves out of fellowship with the Son and the Spirit.

Finally, to the church of the Laodiceans, the Son and the Spirit penetrate to see that here is a lukewarm church. Again, He does not say, "I have somewhat against thee." He makes it even more specific: "I am so much against you that I will spue you out of my mouth." It is even suggested here that the whole church at Laodicea had become lukewarm. What was happening? They were attempting to contain the two extremes — hot and cold. Result — they became lukewarm. Extremes dilute one another. It is still true that Christ and Belial have nothing in common. Hot and cold have nothing in common. They only dilute each other and make an insipid lukewarmness.

One can look at all of these and find the residue still evident in today's churches. The fact of the matter is the first six added up create number seven. When the church has lost her first love and there is perversion in it, a lack of nonconformity, the presence of false teaching, the desire for flexibility and hypocrisy, there can be nothing but lukewarmness. The Son and the Spirit penetrate the real condition of the church.

I would like to call attention to a recent issue of *Christianity Today* in which Otto F. Stahlke wrote under the title, "The New Syncretistic Dialogue." He exposed in that article published December 3, 1971, the underworkings of the World Council of Churches and how a new approach to the syncretization of religion is on the way. The last two paragraphs of his article may point up for us the necessity of the prophetic work of the Holy Spirit in this penetrating way.

"In many parts of the world a tolerant pluralism is not easily achieved. Yet a growing enlightenment in many countries may promise a greater toleration, if in the interest of national progress the governments allow the freedom of worship that the principles of pluralistic democracy imply. Evangelical leaders have the opportunity to make their views known to national leaders, who may show greater confidence in honest churchmanship than in the syncretism of a moribund ecumenism.

"The words of Stephen Neill in *Call to Mission* (Fortress, 1970) remind the church of its abiding task: 'The missionary must have no doubt as to the purpose for which he has come overseas. He must be a missionary. That means that, waking or sleeping, he must be dominated by one central concern — that men and women should be brought to know Jesus Christ and to find life in Him.' " *Christianity Today*, December 3, 1971, p. 221.

We should clearly and quickly see that God is not deluded. The Son and the Spirit can penetrate to the real depth of the life of the church.

III. *The Son and the Spirit Remonstrate*

We must return now to examine the letters to the seven churches once again from another standpoint. After the Lord of the church penetrated the real condition of the seven churches, He had a further word for them. We find in five of the churches the call to repentance. Let us note that with Ephesus the word was, "repent, or else I will remove thy candlestick, thy lampstand, out of its place." The church at Ephesus under a threat of losing her position as a church was called to repentance. They had left their first love. They were not worthy to stay in their place unless they came to repentance.

To the church at Pergamos the remonstrance was, "repent, or else I will come unto thee quickly and will fight against thee with the sword of my mouth." He who stood before them, having the sharp sword with two edges, threatened them, that unless they returned to the biblical position of nonconformity, He would fight against them with the sword of His mouth. It would be a losing battle for them, to be sure.

To the church at Thyatira, the warning came, she did not repent and because she did not repent, "I will cast her into a bed, and them that commit adultery with her into great tribulation, except they repent of their deeds." False doctrine carries with it the threat of great tribulation. It may be that some then, as now, believed they could make necessary accommodations for the existing society and get by. But the Lord says they can't. Will you note that the further call is, "Hold fast till I come"?

To the church at Sardis, the Lord said, "If you do not repent, I will come as a thief and you won't know what hour I am coming and I will catch you unprepared." To them He also said, "Hold fast what you have."

To the church at Philadelphia, He urged, "Hold fast."

To the church at Laodicea He said, "Be zealous therefore, and repent." If you do not, "I will spue you out of my mouth," — complete and utter rejection.
152

The Son and the Spirit remonstrate. The word to the church is repent, return to where you were. Change your mind and come back. If you do not change your mind, if you do not repent, then the threat of the extinguished lampstand, of having to face the Lord with a sharp two-edged sword, to be cast into great tribulation, to be taken unawares, or even to be spued out will be the result.

You will note too that to Thyatira, to Sardis and to Philadelphia, He said, "Hold fast." Sometimes what one hears in the charismatic movement is, "Now that you have been blessed by the Spirit, you can let go of this or this or this. These are no longer important. You can let go of these." But the prophetic work of the Holy Spirit, the lessons we learn from these messages to the seven churches is, "Hold fast, hold fast."

We must quickly see that real division comes under the analysis and the remonstrance of the Son and the Spirit. There are only two sides. You are either with Him or you stand against Him. God is not diverted. He will not turn aside from the path of truth as it is in Him. You can't let go of divine truth without coming under the remonstrance of the Son and the Spirit, if it be true to Revelation 2 and 3.

IV. *The Son and the Spirit Compensate*

Our fourth lesson is common to all of the churches. The promise is made by the Lord of the church and endorsed by the Spirit that compensation is going to come to the overcomer. He is going to receive far more than he expected. With the Ephesian church promise is made that at last the overcomer will have access to the tree of life. He will receive fruit from

153

the tree of life in the midst of the paradise of God.

The overcomer in the Smyrna church will receive the crown of life and the second death will have no hurt for him.

The overcomer in the church at Pergamos will have the privilege of eating of the hidden manna, will have a white stone and a new name written in it, which no one knows but he himself.

The overcomer in the church of Thyatira will have share over the nations to rule them with a rod of iron and he will receive the morning star.

The overcomer in the church of Sardis will be clothed in white raiment and have his name confessed before the Father and before the holy angels.

The overcomer in the church at Philadelphia will become a pillar in the temple of God and have complete security with a new name, access to the city of God.

The overcomer in the church of Laodicea will rule with Christ in His throne.

The Son and the Spirit compensate with the tree of life, the crown of life, the hidden manna, the ruling rod, the blessed acknowledgment, the complete security, and co-regency with Jesus.

God is not deceptive. What He promises He will do. Let those who are undergoing great trial take comfort and assurance from these compensations.

Conclusion

We must learn, therefore, from Revelation 2 and 3 the following lessons on the prophetic work of the Spirit.

The Son and the Spirit cooperate. What one says or

does the other supports. Furthermore, God's Word is a part of that unity. The Godhead is not divided.

The Son and the Spirit know the exact state of each local assembly. No one can gloss over the real situation. The burning eyes of the Lord of the church can penetrate the best attempts of men to cover up. The Godhead is not deluded.

The Son and the Spirit will not tolerate evil in the church. Unrepentant attitudes bring severe judgment upon the guilty. They remonstrate the church and call to repentance, to steadfastness, and the defense of the truth. There is no room for containment of extremes. The Godhead is not diverted.

The overcomer is assured a rich reward including all from which man has been barred since the days of Eden. At last he will have right to the tree of life, he will receive the crown of life, he will stand in the presence of God, he will share in the total dominion of the Perfect God-Man, when He rules the nations with the rod of iron. The Son and the Spirit compensate. The Godhead is not deceptive. Thus the prophetic work of the Spirit is in complete harmony with the prophetic work of the Son and the total work of the Godhead and the complete disclosure of the revelation of God. Amen.

10

THE
HOLY SPIRIT
AND
CHURCH
ADMINISTRATION

By Sanford G. Shetler

The relative scarcity of resource materials on the Holy Spirit and church administration makes us wonder just how important this phase of the doctrine of the Holy Spirit is in the minds of Bible students. In the list of Spirit manifestations mentioned in 1 Corinthians 12:4-6 we are reminded that there are different kinds of gifts or gracious endowments (charismata); different kinds of services, aids and offices in the church (diakonia); and different kinds of operations of an unusual order (energemata). All of these relate directly to the second list of Spirit-manifestations mentioned in the latter part of the chapter. Paul says that to every one is given some manifestation of the Spirit which enables him to be fruitful in his own way in the Christian life and in the life of the church. None of these is for the personal gratification of the possessor but for the benefit of all believers and for those who are not believers. Interestingly, whereas these gifts represent total service to the total church, they also represent ministration to the total man. The "helps" and "governments" mentioned toward the end of this second list in 1 Corinthians seem to belong to the category of Spirit-manifestations known as *diakonia* (ministry or service).

Our immediate concern then in this topic is to look at the relation of those persons who are called "helpers" and "administrators," to use the words of the translators in the Revised Standard Version.

As in the other areas relating to the Holy Spirit, there is a temptation here today to start by relating personal experiences in Holy Spirit leading in administration. For no less than in the matter of infilling or in the ecstatic manifestations, one can recall many marvelous experiences in which the Spirit has also led in the organizing and administrative work of the church. I wish I had the time here to relate some of my own experiences in which the Holy Spirit so clearly led. But to bypass all of the rich Bible background in both Testaments, is simply to short-circuit our understanding of the doctrine of the Holy Spirit. Furthermore, to lay aside the total teaching of the Scriptures, relying only on subjective experience for our source of information, is at the least a precarious procedure. Just as precarious is it to attempt to *interpret* the Scriptures on the basis of personal experience.

The Holy Spirit's relationships, as unfolded in the Bible, include the cosmic order, the church and its leadership, the individual believer, and the Godhead itself. In this particular discussion we are attempting to deal with the Spirit's specific relationship to administration in the church. We want to approach this by looking at the following:

I. *Old Testament typology — the Holy Anointing Oil*
II. *Administration as a Gift of the Spirit*
III. *The Holy Spirit as Administrator*
IV. *The Holy Spirit in Administration*

I. Old Testament Typology — the Holy Anointing Oil

In Exodus 30 the Lord gave Moses precise instructions on the compounding of holy anointing oil. Oil in Bible figurative language represents the Holy Spirit. The oil was to be composed of the spices: myrrh, cinnamon, calamus, and cassia, compounded with olive oil, all in exact proportions. All of these spices were sweet-smelling, a type of the Holy Spirit's grace in the New Testament. In Acts we read: "Great grace was upon all." The holy anointing oil was to be used to anoint the tabernacle and its appointments and Aaron and his sons, who were to be consecrated for the *"priest's office"* (administration). When the oil was applied to Aaron and his sons it was a sign that they were set apart to the priesthood and qualified therefor. They were told also

> Upon man's flesh shall it not be poured, neither shall ye make any other like it, after the composition of it; it is holy, and it shall be holy unto you.
> Whosoever compoundeth any like it, or whosoever putteth any of it upon a stranger, shall . . . be cut off from his people (Ex. 30:32, 33).

In short, there can never be any concourse between flesh and Spirit, there can be no substitute for the Holy Spirit, and no "stranger" or unconverted person, is eligible for the receiving of the Spirit. To amplify this, no human or fleshly qualities of leadership, or any other form of human organization, can ever take the place of the presence and power of the Spirit. Arthur W. Climenhaga, speaking on this point at the Mennonite World Conference at Amsterdam, 1967, the theme of which was "The Witness of the Spirit," said,

> The church that is "man-managed" instead of Spirit-governed is doomed to spiritual failure. A ministry that is theologically trained but not Spirit-filled works no miracles. The church that multiplies committees but neglects the life of the Spirit may be noisy and enterprising or quiet and subdued, but it labors in vain and spends its strength for nothing. It is possible to excel in mechanics and fail in dynamic. There is a superabundance of machinery; what is wanting is power. And thus while man can supply the energy, enterprise, and enthusiasm for human organization, the real work of the church depends upon the power of the Spirit.

It has been said frequently — and correctly — that in many churches today the Holy Spirit could leave without any discernible difference. Like Sardis, a church may have all the outward characteristics of a live, well-organized church, and yet, without the Spirit, be dead. Quoting Climenhaga again,

> Thus in our consideration of the church and the Spirit we declare that for much that is undertaken by the church the Holy Spirit is not needed. Religious services

and organized institutions do not necessarily constitute a Christian church and such may flourish without the activity of the Holy Spirit in their midst.

To summarize very briefly, one can say unequivocally, that from the leadership down (or up!) only those anointed by the Spirit of God can be considered as having the proper credentials for service in the church, and only through such service will their work be acceptable and effective.

II. Administration as a Gift of the Spirit

In the passage in 1 Corinthians 12:14-31 we have a clear description of the church operating as the human body in an orderly and organized way, each member contributing to the total functioning of the body. At the close of this passage, as mentioned earlier, "helps" and "governments" are mentioned as gifts (or functions) of the Spirit. "And God has appointed in the church first apostles; second, prophets; third, teachers; then workers of miracles, then healers, helpers, *administrators*, speakers in various tongues. Are all apostles? Are all prophets? Are all teachers? Do all work miracles? Do all possess gifts of healing? Do all speak with tongues? Do all interpret? But earnestly desire the higher gifts" (RSV, v. 28). Note that there is suggested here a priority of gifts, and that in this priority, administration is lower than "prophets" or "teachers." Without pushing this idea of priority too far, it does seem that in the list of services in the church, administration is not rated as high as we rate it today. Administrative positions were never to be regarded as power and prestige positions, but as functional roles, geared to making the whole body operate harmoniously and effectively. A position or office is to be respected not for the prestige men may invest in it, but for the fruitful service it represents. Paul wrote: "And we beseech you, brethren, to know them which labour among you, and are over you in the Lord, and admonish you; and to esteem them very highly in love *for their work's sake*" (1 Thess. 5:12).

Organization for the sake of organization, one of the earmarks of much of modern Christendom, is an impediment to the full working of the Spirit. There are always those, who like Diotrephes, mentioned the third Epistle of John, "love to have the preeminence," or, as one version puts it, "Who [are] eager to be leader[s]." We are all too ready, it seems, to draw elaborate organizational charts with the neat boxes and circles and vertical and horizontal lines showing the chain of command — or to borrow a term used to describe the bird kingdom, to establish the "pecking order." Impressive as all this may appear to the leadership itself, the laity, who is far more concerned in having dedicated administration at the grassroots level, than in recognizing positions of eminence, remains unimpressed. This idea of *dedicated leadership that serves* is reinforced in Paul's letter to Timothy, when he writes, "Let the elders who rule well be considered worthy of double honor, *especially those who labor in preaching and teaching.*" The New English Bible renders this as follows: "Elders who do well as *leaders* are worthy of a double stipend."

III. The Holy Spirit as Administrator

Having looked briefly at the place of "government" or administration in the list of gifts and services, let us go on now to the specific work of the Spirit *as* church administrator.

James Green, in his *Studies in the Holy Spirit,* a book which has been a source book for me in my studies in the Holy Spirit for many years, says, "If Christ is the authority over the church, the Spirit is the authority within the church." He quotes A. T. Pierson, who often spoke of the "presidency of the Spirit," a very apt phrase. He, the Holy Spirit, "presides over the affairs of the church He formed [and] occupies and animates it."

This phase of the Spirit's office may be abundantly illustrated from the Acts of the Apostles.

It was the Spirit, for example, who staffed the church. (Acts 6, 13, and 20.) This involved men for different roles and services. Those who looked after material matters were called by the Spirit.

> "Wherefore, brethren, look ye out among you seven men of honest report, full of the Holy Ghost and wisdom, whom we may appoint over this business [or duty]" (6:3).

The movement now called foreign missions was inaugurated not by man but by the Spirit of God.

> "As they ministered to the Lord, and fasted, *the Holy Ghost said, Separate me Barnabas and Saul for the work whereunto I have called them*" (Acts 13:2).

In Acts 20 we note that likewise overseers or elders were called by the Spirit.

"Take heed therefore unto yourselves, and to all the flock, over the which *the Holy Ghost hath made you overseers* [RSV: guardians] to feed [shepherd] the church of God, which he hath purchased with his own blood" (20:28).

Weidner, in his *Biblical Theology of the New Testament* (Fleming H. Revell Co., New York, p. 198), says

"The right government of the church depends, above all, on the right appointment of office-bearers, which consists of bishops and deacons, and in the administration of proper discipline."

Biblical instructions of Holy Spirit direction in the administration of the church also include the story of the first general conference in church history (Acts 15). The conference was called to consider the terms of admission of Gentiles to membership in the church. In this historic meeting the Spirit is recognized as the wisdom of the meeting, the real author of its decisions.

"For it seemed good to the Holy Ghost, and to us, to lay upon you no greater burden than these necessary things" (Acts 15:28).

One might spend considerable time at this point to discuss the implications of the Holy Spirit in conference deliberations and decisions. Green says,

"Whether we think of the church as an organism, or an organization, the Spirit is the principle of its life, the board of its unity (1 Cor. 12:13), the spring of its vitality and vigor, the source of its character, wisdom and ministry (1 Cor. 12:4, 7-11). If the Spirit should leave the church, it would cease to be an organism and an organ, and become only an organization. . . .

163

The Spirit is the dynamic of the Christian life, whether in the individual or in the community [of believers]. He is the *personal directive agency in the church.*"

The Spirit's role *as* Administrator is shown also in His leading men to the right place at the right time to make their work most effective. Classic examples of this are found in the cases of Philip and the Ethiopian and of Peter and Cornelius (Acts 9 and 10). Like an administrator issuing executive orders, the Spirit said to Philip, "Go join thyself to this chariot," and to Peter, "Behold, three men seek thee. Arise therefore, and get thee down, and go with them, doubting nothing: for I have sent them."

Proper choice, ultilization, and deployment of personnel is always considered the mark of a good administrator. In this the Spirit is superb.

IV. *The Holy Spirit in Administration*

Coming now to our last division, What are the specific duties of a church administrator which call for the Holy Spirit's guidance and direction? The Holy Spirit certainly works through a spiritual administrator. One may list three general categories:

(1) Routine administrative duties.

(2) As a manager of God's truth (1 Cor. 4:1).

(3) As a manager of men.

It should be remembered, of course, that there is no real division between the Holy Spirit *as* Administrator and His role *in* administration. For, if He is given proper place, He will still serve *as* Administrator — *as* the *president* or *presiding elder* of the church. It is rather for the purpose of discussion that we separate the human function from the divine role, keeping in

164

mind, however, that in the ideal situation the two merge into one.

(1) *Routine Administrative Duties*

In this category one might place the many pastoral duties, worship services, baptisms, communions, services on committees, financial leadership, conference work, etc. In reality, of course, no routine duty is ever routine, if the Holy Spirit is in it. Every baptism, for example, should be a new, fresh experience. The planning and programming and timing of church calendar activities can all be lifted out of the level of the routine to that of the extraordinary, making the least more effective and fruitful.

A word about the worship service. Just how far should the administrator go in structuring this? Someone has pointed out that of all Christians, Quakers have left the most opportunity for the Spirit to work in the worship service. They act as if they believed that the Spirit was really present and presiding. Their services are not arranged beforehand.

Green says, "If the worship of the church had been less rigid and frigid, there would have been less reason for the protest of the Quietists, Mystics, Friends, and Brethren of whom we read in church history."

A. J. Gordon wrote years ago, "Honor the Holy Spirit as Master of Assemblies; study much the secret of surrender to Him: be submissive to keep silence when He forbids, as well as to speak when He commands, and we shall learn how much better is God's way of conducting the worship of His house than man's way."

This matter of structuring church services raises, of

165

course, the whole matter of structuring in the work of the church. Just how far can planning and structuring go in the whole church program? The matter of decision-making is another matter of concern that falls under this category of routine work. What place does "democracy" have in the church? The matter of determining when to make a single-handed administrative decision and when to put a matter before the church to vote is always itself a matter for administrative decision. Are there times when the Spirit leads directly through the spiritual overseer and times when His will is revealed through the body? To sense when the channels are open one way or the other is alone a task that requires spiritual discernment. On this point Wayne Oates writes,

> The modern pastor cannot be too much of a purist about "not using power" in human relationships . . . the struggle of the soul of the Christian administrator is to know *when* to use power in behalf of his organization, and *how* to avoid "lording it over" those to whom he is called as an "example unto the flock" (*The Five Worlds of the Holy Spirit*, p. 111).

It is a temptation for a pastor or an administrator who has built up a good rapport with his people to influence them unduly in the direction of his own thinking without involving them sufficiently in the decision-making process. Or, contrariwise, there is also a temptation to abdicate his leadership rights for the sake of popularity, following his flock where they would lead him.

The matter of raising money is another administrative duty that can hardly be carried on without Holy

Spirit direction. In this it is so easy to resort to human methods and give it a Holy Spirit label. Can one legitimately put on crusades in the name of the Holy Spirit, when part of the machinery itself involves some men and means that are less than Holy Spirit in-filled and guided? Should unregenerate men, for example, ever be involved in the process? Can men who are not Christians be solicited for funds? Just what is or is not Holy-Spirit-inspired giving? The allocation of funds also becomes a matter for administrative decision at one level or another. How can this be done so that one can clearly see the place of the Spirit? Still another task in the course of routine duty is that of "filling positions." This can so easily be carried out without feeling the presence of the Spirit. But should there be any less concern and ceremony in filling, for example, the position of janitor than in consecrating a Sunday-school superintendent or a pastor to his task? Are there levels of holiness in terms of positions?

(2) *The Administrator as a Manager of God's Truth*

In 1 Corinthians 4:1 Paul wrote, "Let a man so account of us as of the ministers of Christ, and *stewards* of the mysteries of God." The Emphasized New Testament translates the word stewards as *officers,* and Goodspeed translates the same word as *managers:* "As managers authorized to distribute the secret truths of God." In the next verse, which reads in the King James Version: "Moreover it is required in stewards, that a man be found faithful," the Phillips translation reads as follows: "And it is a prime requisite in a *trustee* that he should prove worthy of his trust." Significantly, the words *stewards,*

167

managers, officers, and *trustees* all suggest administrative roles. In short, it is one of the chief tasks of the church administrator, under the direction of the Holy Spirit, to act as a trustee or manager of God's truth. It is a function that cannot be carried lightly.

Weidner, mentioned earlier, under the topic of "The Church and Church Government," refers to 1 Tim. 3:15, where the church is characterized as the "pillar and ground of the truth," and says, "God is the Master of this holy household (2 Tim. 2:21); its stewards are the bishops or pastors. (Tit. 1:7) . . ." The most important interest of the [pastoral] Epistles he says is "how doctrine is to be kept pure for the future in the church. . . ." The disciples were to look out for trustworthy men, and to commission these with the work of teaching.

Acts 20, also referred to earlier, gives us the relationship of the Holy Spirit to this work of serving as *managers* or *trustees* of God's truth.

"Take heed therefore unto yourselves, and to all the flock, over the which the Holy Ghost hath made you overseers (RSV: "guardians"), to feed [or shepherd] the church of God, which he hath purchased with his own blood. For I know this, that after my departing shall grievous wolves enter in among you, not sparing the flock. Also of your own selves shall men arise, speaking perverse things, to draw away disciples after them. Therefore watch, and remember, that by the space of three years I ceased not to warn every one night and day with tears."

Today this role of serving as custodian or guardian of the mysteries or the "great truths of God" does not seem to have the respect it had in the days of the great apologists. To attempt to "earnestly contend for the faith which was once delivered unto the saints" is not a popular role today. Nevertheless, in the list of the *charismata* is also the gift of *discernment*. Why is it that in the quest for a charismatic experience so little is made of this gift today? Though perhaps far less spectacular, the church of our time certainly needs the exercise of this gift no less than it was needed in the days of the early church.

I once asked one of the very successful administrators in our church, now gone to his reward, what he considered one of the important responsibilities of a pastor or bishop. He said, "Watch who you bring into your pulpit." There was a time when Mennonites were strict in their selection of guest speakers — so strict, in fact, that scarcely anyone *but* a Mennonite was allowed to speak and not every Mennonite was welcomed. While this kind of custodianship may seem a bit rigid or stuffy, yet today it seems we have almost gone overboard in the other direction, being frequently not too selective in whom we ask or permit to speak. This, of course, would be but one application of this idea, but *we are responsible to serve as trustworthy managers of God's truth.*

The third category of duties of an administrator which calls for Spirit guidance is that of being a (3) *Manager of Men.*

As stated earlier, the choice and deployment of personnel is always an important function of administration.

Wayne Oates writes on this point:

> As custodian of gifts, a spiritual overseer has the responsibility of recognizing the varieties of gifts within

the flock of God, appreciating the varieties of services, perceiving the varieties of workings. [He refers here to the charismata, diakonia, and energemata.] He must have the grace and compassion, the overview and perception, to see that each is given the manifestation of the Spirit for the common good. (1 Cor. 12:7.)

In God's program no one is expendable and no one is indispensable. Impartiality and common courtesy go a long way in seeking out and recognizing gifts in others. It is so easy to deliberately bypass individuals who seem less desirable to us or with whom, perhaps, we have found some difficulty in agreeing. The good administrator will never let personal animosities or bad memories interfere with the full workings of the Spirit. Paul, who had one time had some difficulty with John Mark, later found him very useful (2 Tim. 4:11).

One of the abiding problems in church work is that of personnel management. Keeping the wheels of a church or conference or church institution turning is not one of the easiest tasks of an administrator, since we are dealing with many and varied individuals. Paul, with all of his firmness for truth, was also tender and compassionate toward those he served. His ability to work with men, and his professional courtesy toward colleagues is shown in his affectionate farewell to the elders of Ephesus (Acts 20:17-38). His personal devotion in service and his close contact with other leaders was marked. He was never an administrator to issue orders from a central office like an army field commander, but he literally — that is personally — covered every part of the territory in which he served from Jerusalem to Yugoslavia. He wrote to the Romans

(Rom. 15:18, 19), "For I will not dare to speak of any of those things which Christ hath not wrought by me, to make the Gentiles obedient, by word and deed, through mighty signs and wonders, by the power of the Spirit of God; so that from Jerusalem, and round about unto Illyricum, I have fully preached the gospel of Christ." Paul was not a detached VIP, but was in the main thrust of the work.

As a church organizer Paul has been unequaled in history. At Corinth less than two years and at Thessalonica probably only three weeks, he was able, under the dynamic influence of the Holy Spirit, to establish churches using at once local talent for his churches. At Ephesus after eighteen months he was able to ordain elders!

An administrator is often like a catalyst serving to stimulate others to be the most effective, himself sometimes almost submerged or hidden. At the best he must depend upon the Holy Spirit's presence and that is why it is so important to have the Spirit operative in the lives of *all* the members of the body of Christ. For no matter how much the leaders of a church are infilled by the Spirit, their work can only be effective if the total church is found walking and living in the Spirit.

The matter of resolving conflict comes under the management of men. This is more than is often conceived, an exercise in human diplomacy. Direct confrontation, probably the least desired means of resolving conflict, may be exactly the method which the Spirit can use best. This is beautifully illustrated in the Jerusalem Conference. Church discipline is an administrative function. First Corinthians 5 gives us an

171

example of the administrator taking the initiative in the act, assigning the function to the gathered group. The binding and loosing function (Mt. 18:17, 18) is an administrative function.

Too often the administrator finds his work cut out for him and finds himself merely trying to fill a position. He should be able to use the structures rather than letting them use him. The administrator of the people of God does have his work cut out for him, but in a different sense. He should always mobilize the administrative structures so as to lead and not merely manipulate people. He must never operate on the level of mere expediency.

At the best, however, he will be criticized for being partial, for bungling, for being too authoritative or not authoritative enough, for being spineless, and of creating credibility gaps. He will fall at times into periods of depression and to what has been called "executive loneliness." Yet the administrator who perceives himself as an undershepherd, a man also under authority, and as a co-laborer with God through the Holy Spirit, never serves in isolation. The great function of the Holy Spirit is to provide him with the needed companionship.

The main responsibility of making leadership a success still lies with the leader himself.

Titus 1:7. "For a bishop, [or pastor] as God's steward, must be blameless; he must not be arrogant or quick-tempered, or a drunkard, or violent, or greedy for gain, but hospitable, a lover of goodness, master of himself, upright, *holy*, and self-controlled; he must hold firm to the same sure word as taught, so that he may be able to give instruction and also to confute those who contradict it."

In closing I would like to use a quotation from Green. Green, when he speaks of the Spirit in relation to the cosmic order, says He is the great "finisher." He continues:

> "If I may use a figure, the Father furnishes the blueprints, the Son provides the material, and the Spirit erects and adorns the structure and occupies it. . . . Every feather, every leaf, every flower, every fruit, is the Spirit's artistry, the Spirit's workmanship."

And so may I conclude, if a congregation is under the control and direction of the Spirit, that church will be an example of the same kind of artistry and workmanship, *in believers and in their leaders*, making them truly a holy temple unto the Lord.

11

GLOSSOLALIA IN THE CHURCH TODAY

By David Ewert

Any study of the phenomenon known as glossolalia will have to begin with the New Testament. In the entire Book of Acts (the most complete source of information on the early Christian church that we have) there are only three passages that mention speaking in tongues. Chapter 2 appears to stand in a class by itself, for as far as we know, the miracle of Pentecost, by which the apostles were enabled to communicate the gospel to the Pentecost visitors in their native dialects, was never repeated (at least there is no record of it in the New Testament). The speaking in tongues mentioned in chapters 10 and 19 appears to have been an attendant circumstance which on these two occasions (the only two mentioned) marked a breakthrough from darkness to the light of the Christian faith.

Outside of these three references, what we know about glossolalia from the New Testament, comes from the 1 Cor. 12 — 14. Only in these chapters is the matter of speaking in tongues within the life of the Christian community dealt with. For this reason we shall focus our attention on these chapters, particularly on chapter 14. However, we must look at chapters 12 and 13 for one moment to gain perspectives. In conclusion I propose to suggest a few things regarding attitudes toward the charismatic movement today and its interest in glossolalia.

1. Glossolalia in the Corinthian Church

Just how widespread the gift of tongues was in the Corinthian church we do not know, but the exercise of the gift by members of the congregation endangered the unity of the church. Those who had been endowed with this ecstatic gift tended to despise those not so endowed; and those who did not have the gift were jealous of those who spoke in tongues. And so Paul sets about to regulate the use of this charism in the church.

He begins by pointing out to his readers that the real test of the presence of the Spirit in a man's life is whether he confesses Christ as Lord (12:1-3). Ecstasy is not peculiar to Christianity, it can be found in pagan religions also, but where men acknowledge Christ as Lord in their life we have a genuine evidence of the presence of the Spirit.

In 12:4-11 Paul stresses the fact that although God equips people in different ways in order to fulfill their calling in the church, this diversity must never

175

lead to disunity, since all charisms come from the same divine source. God gives to each one of His children gifts which enable them to be of service to others, and not for self-glorification. To be proud of the gifts of grace given to us sovereignly by God is out of order; to be envious of those who have gifts we don't have is equally bad. Nor is it proper for someone endowed with a certain gift to dictate to another that he must have the same gift.

Interestingly, in both lists of *charismata* given in chapter 12 tongues appear last. One wonders whether that is of any significance or not. Moreover, in the list of gifts at the end of the chapter, some of the gifts turn out to be people (the list in Ephesians 4 has people only). Also, some of the gifts listed are not of the ecstatic kind: *anatilympseis* (helps), *kubernesis* (leadership). I suppose Paul wants to say that there is no aspect of the life of the church, where we are not dependent on God's Spirit for help. The rhetorical questions of vv. 29, 30 of 1 Corinthians 12, which demand a "No!" for an answer, make it abundantly clear that not all believers have the same gifts.

Of course where there is little interest in serving Christ, the gifts vanish. It is for this reason, no doubt, that Paul stresses the importance of "being zealous" for the gifts.

Chapter 13 is sandwiched in between the two chapters that deal with gifts in order to show that if love, a fruit of the Spirit, is lacking, spiritual gifts are of no significance at all. For our purposes, at the moment, the conclusion of chapter 13 (vv. 8-13) is most significant. Here the charismatic gifts: prophecy,

176

tongues, gnosis (and by implication all the others) are said to be ephemeral. They are useful for this age only, and since they are given for this age they partake of the imperfections of it. When, however, the *teleion* comes, the consummation, then these gifts with their imperfections will be done away with.

Two illustrations underscore the passing significance of the *charismata*. In childhood one prattles like a child *(laleo)*, one thinks and reasons like a child. With manhood all this changes. So it is with the church. Not that the immature need the charisms and the mature do not; nor that the early church needed the gifts of grace and the later does not. As long as the church is on this earth it needs the *pneumatika* to fulfill its calling; once it reaches the gates of perfection it can dispense with them.

A mirror reflects only an imperfect image, and even when the reflection is good, it is still an indirect way of seeing. As long as we are in this age our vision is somewhat blurred; but in the consummation we shall look directly into His face *(prosopon pros prosopon)*, and then all will be plain. In contrast to all these ephemeral gifts (tongues, prophecy, or any other) love is eternal and therefore of much greater significance.

II. *Glossolalia Vis-a-Vis Prophecy* 14:1-40.

A. The Comparative Value of Tongues and Prophecy (vv. 1-25)

Paul argues that prophecy is superior to tongues for the church (1-19) as well as for the unbeliever (vv. 20-25). He begins by exhorting his readers to pursue *agape*, but to be desirous of *pneumatika* as well. Then

177

the apostle gives his reasons why prophecy is to be preferred to tongues.

1. The Argument, vv. 2-6. The reason *propheteia* is of greater value than tongues is that a man speaking in tongues engages in spiritual soliloquy; he engages in communion between himself and God; it's a mysterious process. But it has no meaning for the congregation, because it is not intelligible. Since speaking in tongues was a bit more flashy, we can see why it was highly desired in Corinth, apparently as a sign of greater spirituality. But Paul says: No one hears him; not that tongues-speaking is not audible, but it is not intelligible (*ecoutes*, but not *entendre*).

Prophecy on the other hand (v. 3) has value for the congregation. By it the congregation (a) is built up — it instructs and inspires; (b) people are comforted (if that is what *paraklesis* means here) — "comfort" perhaps in the Latin sense of *con-fortis* — to be strengthened; (c) they are encouraged (*paramuthia*); there are always people in the congregation who need this kind of ministry, and this often makes preaching so rewarding.

In v. 4 the contrast is seen clearly: the one who speaks in a tongue builds *himself* up, the one who prophesies builds the *congregation* up. Paul admits that he would be quite happy if all spoke in tongues, but much more delighted if they engaged in a prophetic ministry. However, in the case of tongues there is a condition that must be met: that which is spoken must be interpreted if it is to have any meaning for the congregation. (At this point there are at times subtle evasions when people gather in smaller groups to exercise tongues without an in-

178

terpreter, and then say this is private and not public. They forget that in the early period all churches were house-gatherings.)

There is then an important principle to observe in the use of all gifts: Do they build up the congregation? That, of course, would hold true for natural gifts as well. It is exactly in this way that love as the underpinning principle of the Christian life and worship manifests itself.

In v. 6 Paul takes a hypothetical situation to drive home his point. If he should come to them and speak in tongues he would not help them a whole lot unless he communicated some revelation, or insight *(gnosis)* — the communication of it is described as prophecy and teaching. He wants everything that goes on in the worship services of the congregation to be intelligible.

2. The Illustrations, vv. 7-13. The illustrations will show that tongues are inferior to prophecy (in their effect). They are taken from two realms: musical instruments (7-9), and voices (10-13) — deliberately chosen since they are so close to the use of tongues and prophecy.

a. Musical instruments (vv. 7-9). An instrument as such is without life; it is made of wood, steel, brass, bone, or what have you (that goes for both the winds and the strings). But they come to life when a meaningful variation of sound is made; when the musician strikes the strings the instrument communicates a message.

When an army is to move, the message of the bugler, the trumpet, must sound the proper note, or else they will be confused about the signal. If a trumpet blast is to serve as a sign, a signal, it must be intelligible. The application (v. 9) is obvious. If a man speaks in a tongue and the words are not *eusemos* (intelligible), i.e., easy, well, plus *semaino* (cf. semantics) — signify. If people can't understand them, he speaks into the air, and that is devastating criticism.

b. Human speech (vv. 10-13). There are many kinds of *phonai* (languages, sounds, noises, voices) in the world, i.e., in existence, and every one has its meaning, its signification. None is *aphonos*. All of us here know English and so we can communicate; if I should speak in a language that you did not understand, I would be to you a *barbaros* (onomatopoeic word) — derogatory term for uncivilized people who in Paul's age didn't speak Greek.

Paul drives home the application in v. 12. Since they are such zealots for spiritual gifts, they should not forget that their main function is to build up the church, and it is in this that they should excel (*perisseuo*). For this reason, if a man who has the gift of tongues wants to exercise this gift, then he must pray for an additional gift: that of interpretation.

3. The Personal Example, vv. 14-19. Using himself as an example, Paul says that when he prays in a tongue his spirit prays, but his mind is unfruitful. "My spirit" could mean (a) his inner makeup (but non-intellectual); (b) spiritual gift; or (c) the Holy Spirit given to him. In any case, it is not a praying with the mind, the intellect (a kind of praying that is perfectly legitimate) — whether spontaneous or memorized.

Paul says he will pray both ways (v. 15); with the spirit, and with the mind; i.e., charismatically and normally; not that one is more spiritual than the other, but the one may lift up the soul in private devotion, whereas the other profits also those who hear us pray; the kind of praying that is to be done in public.

This goes for singing as well (*psallo* — to begin with meant to pluck the strings, then to accompany, and then to sing). This could mean that there was ecstatic singing as well as praying, or else that the ecstatic praying had musical characteristics.

If Paul should pray in a tongue publicly, then the uninitiated (*idiotes*) would not even be able to say "Amen" after the prayer (a custom fast disappearing; it was a synagogue practice) for he doesn't know what was said. With a bit of irony he says (v. 17) that it is a very nice prayer that you are offering to God, but if the other person is not built up, it's of no use to him, because he can't understand.

Now, just to make sure that no one gets the idea that Paul is minimizing the value of tongues, because he doesn't have the gift, and that this is sour grapes, he reminds them that he has the gift; but in the congregation he refuses to use it, since he is concerned with edification. He would rather speak five words with the mind, i.e., the kind that people can understand, than a torrent of nonsense syllables.

B. For the Unbeliever, vv. 20-25

Before informing the readers on how the speaking in tongues and the prophesying affect the unbelievers, he exhorts them to be done with childish things and to grow up: "Stop becoming children in the mind." Children are interested in the sensational, the spectacular. There is of course an area in which wholesome naivete is in place, that is in the experience and knowledge of evil.

But now to the argument: in the law, i.e., the Old Testament, it is written (Is. 28:11, Paul quotes freely from the LXX): "I will speak through strange tongues and by the lips of foreigners, but they will not listen to me." These are God's words of judgment spoken through the prophet to apostate Israel. Meaning: Because Israel would not listen to the prophets (who spoke their language) they would be judged by foreigners who spoke a different language (Assyrian).

As tongues of foreign powers are to Israel a sign of judgment, so tongues in the church can be a sign of judgment for the unbeliever. It's a sign of division between the believers and unbelievers; the unbeliever sees that he's an outsider; he's not part of the people of God. (Another view is that "unbelievers" here refers to Old Testament unbelievers, but I can't follow that; neither should we infer from the illustration that Paul is dealing here with languages.) Interestingly, Paul does assume that some unbelievers may be present in the church. To the believer, prophecy is a sign — a sign that God is present; He is speaking to them, they can hear Him, signifying that they are the people of God.

However (v. 23), tongues can have another effect on both the unbeliever and the *idiotes* (uninitiated man), and that is the loss of respect for the church (*maino* — maniac). If they should all speak in tongues he will think they are out of their mind. What's the possible effect of prophecy (v. 24)? If an unbeliever or uninitiated man comes to the assembly and hears

182

prophecy (Paul here assumes the work of God's Spirit), he is convicted and he begins to examine himself, sees his condition, and finally he falls upon his face (Oriental gesture), and says, as it were, "God be merciful to me a sinner," and confesses Christ as Lord. The end result will be that such hearers go from the Christian assembly with the deep conviction that God is present (the least we should expect from our worship services).

As far as the effect of tongues on the unbelievers is concerned, there are, then, two possible effects: They may be taken aback when they see that there is something they have not got; or they may lose their respect for the church when they witness the believers in this kind of ecstasy and confusion. Prophecy, on the other hand, is God's Word to believers and unbelievers.

B. The Orderly Employment of Tongues and Prophecy vv. 26-33a

1. General principle, v. 26. We are given some insight into early Christian gatherings. Since they met in homes, naturally the meetings were more casual and spontaneous and there was more active participation of those in attendance. One might recite a psalm, another a teaching (could be an Old Testament text read and explained, or some truth discovered and shared) another an apocalypsis, that is, a new insight which he shares. If someone speaks ecstatically in a tongue, then there must be in interpreter to translate this into intelligible speech.

But in all this spontaneity, and variety, there must be one overarching concern: The upbuilding of the church, a principle which Paul reiterates several

183

times. Incidentally, the concern for the welfare of the church is a safer indication of the fullness of the Spirit than the ability to speak in tongues.

2. Specific instructions, vv. 27-36. (a) Regarding tongues in public, vv. 27, 28. During one service no more than two or three are to exercise the gift and that *ana meros* — by shares, i.e., by turns, each having a fair share of the time — suggests that at times two spoke at once and that at times some speaker dominated the assembly. Another principle to observe is that unless the ecstatic tongues are interpreted for the congregation, they are not to be exercised at all in public. They may be used for private devotions, when the individual believer has communion with God. In church, however, only that which is understood has a place. (b) Regarding prophecy, vv. 29-33a. Preaching/teaching must also be regulated — again no more than two or three at one service (as much as most people can endure anyway). But this does not mean the others are inactive: they are to discern. The latter exercise was important where prophets might get carried away in enthusiasm and say things that brought embarrassment to the church (and that still happens) — it is therefore wiser to prepare ahead of time.

Here it seems as if the prophetic utterances were given spontaneously, and so, courtesy in the sharing of time is to be observed; all prophets are to get an opportunity to address the congregation in order to instruct it and to exhort it. Variety will lead to the fuller edification of the church.

That prophecy (and tongues for that matter) was not an uncontrollable ecstatic condition can be seen in that Paul sees no difficulty in observing good order, since the spirits of the prophets are under the control of the prophets (preparation beforehand, of course, helps in this respect).

Paul concludes these instructions on the use of tongues and prophecy in public by reminding the believers that God is not a God of confusion (*akatastasia*), but of peace, i.e., order. The spontaneous element in Christian worship is not necessarily disorder; on the other hand, let us not deceive ourselves into thinking that when the unexpected happens every Sunday morning that we are then more spiritual (it could be the result of laziness and bad planning).

There follows now a paragraph on the place of the woman in the church, and some concluding remarks on the authority of the instructions which Paul has just given (vv. 37-40). In keeping with the argument of the whole chapter Paul encourages them to be zealous for the prophetic gift but since tongues are also God's gift to the church, they are not to be condemned. In public worship, however, nothing is to happen which would destroy decorum (*euchsemonos*) and order (*taxis*).

III. Glossolalia and Our Attitudes

A. Inherent Dangers in the Current Charismatic Movement

One danger in all renewal movements is that those who experience God in a new way want to live from these experiences. But since we are still in this age and in the flesh, we must walk by faith even in the midst of frustrations, trials, tears, and the shadow of death (cf. 2 Cor. 1). We know, too, that our emotional life cannot be held at a high pitch constantly. The effort to do this often leads to psychic exhaustion and to an erratic kind of Christian life.

Another danger arising out of this emphasis on experience (and, in one sense, we can never emphasize experience enough), is that we make our experience normative for others. This is particularly the case when believers, who have lived on a lower level of Christian life for years, suddenly experience a breakthrough and a transformation of their life through the work of the Holy Spirit. They then tend to think that all believers must experience Christ in this way. Indeed, they search for Scripture texts to substantiate their experience, and this leads, at times, to a misuse of Scripture passages. The only proper term for such a post-conversion crisis experience (and there is no description of such an experience in the New Testament) is that of the "filling" of the Spirit. Our interest in correct biblical terminology should, however, not close our eyes to the reality and meaningfulness of transforming Christian experiences.

B. Attitudes We Should Foster in the Light of the Charismatic Movement

Since the charismatic movement is, in a sense, a reaction toward the indifference and coldness of many professing Christians of various denominations, we should ask serious questions of ourselves with respect to the vitality of our own Christian experience. Then, too, we must cultivate a magnanimous spirit. Just because there have been excesses among the so-called charismatics; just because some who speak in tongues have occasionally made themselves obnoxious; just because the charismatic movement has led to serious disruptions in the life of some congregations, we must be careful not to condemn the movement out of hand as heresy. We know that in all such movements the spurious and the genuine often get mixed up, and that we cannot always distinguish between the authentic and the imitated and induced experiences. Paul's argument in 1 Corinthians 12 is, that the unity of the church is not destroyed by diversity. This means that we must be big enough to accept people with different kinds of spiritual gifts and experiences. Our concern should be that all members use their gifts to serve God and to build His kingdom.

However, those who have the gift of tongues should remember that, without love, "tongues" mean nothing. Often, today, one notices a greater willingness on the part of some believers to accept those who speak in tongues, than on the part of the charismatics to accept those who do not speak in tongues, equally as their brothers and sisters in Christ. The main thrust of 1 Corinthians 12 — 14 is to guard against divisions in the Christian community. When these members within a congregation who have the gift of tongues get off by themselves to exercise their gift, the potential for schism in the Christian community is very real.

Openness to what God is saying to the church through the charismatic movement does not exempt the church from being discerning (which, incidentally, is also a gift of the Spirit).

Let us not be blind to the fact that many lives have been completely transformed by what is sometimes called (wrongly) the "baptism in the Spirit." If our spiritual pilgrimage has been different, let us not be so prejudiced that we cannot discern God's grace in different and, perhaps, unusual ways. The "charismatics," on the other hand, should develop a sense of history, and not presume to have discovered something that the church throughout its history has not known. Peter, in the only passage in which he uses the word *charisma* (and the only passage outside of Paul), exhorts us: "As each has received a gift, employ it for one another, as good stewards of God's varied grace" (1 Pet. 4:10). May this be our constant concern!

12

THE
HOLY SPIRIT
AT WORK
AS
PREDICTED
IN THE GOSPEL
OF JOHN

Introduction

By John R. Mumaw

The Gospel of John is called "the high-water mark" of New Testament teaching on the Holy Spirit. The church's thinking about the Spirit is highly flavored by concepts expressed in John's Gospel.[1] It contains the most clear doctrinal statements about the Spirit found anywhere in the New Testament. And the most precious promises regarding the Holy Spirit are expressed in this Gospel. One seldom talks about Him without some reference (direct or indirect) to John's testimony.

This Gospel of John has also been called "the spiritual Gospel." John deals very intimately with matters pertaining to the Spirit as they relate to the inner life of the believer. The earlier chapters of the Gospel refer more specifically to the Spirit's relation to the individual believer and his personal life. The second part deals more particularly with the Spirit's work in the church. More is said there about the relation of the Spirit to the Christian brotherhood. The upper room discourse especially emphasizes the issues involved in corporate relationships. There we are introduced to the work of the Spirit in the church and to the way He functions in group action.

It must be remembered the Gospel was written after Pentecost. Since the teachings of Christ about the Spirit were given prior to His death and resurrection, we hear His words and the comments of John as predictive messages. They are recorded as having a forward look. We read them as being given in the future tense. So what had future meaning to them has current significance for us. It is this point of view that prevails in this paper.

The significance of the teachings about the Holy Spirit in the Gospel of John is not always recognized in current discussions. Those who rely primarily upon experience to formulate their theology of the Holy Spirit rest their case on the Book of Acts. For a broader base in understanding the work of the Spirit we need the Gospels, especially the teachings of Jesus. The larger doctrinal perspective is seen in this "Gospel of Spiritual Insight." What we find here is basic to our understanding of the person and work of the Spirit as recorded in Acts and the Epistles.

A. The Work of the Spirit in Individual Believers

The Gospel of John deals with the work of the Spirit as it affects the inner life of man. The references to His presence and power in the first thirteen chapters speak directly to what happens to an individual who believes in Jesus Christ. The Holy Spirit comes to us today in Christ Jesus, "That the blessing of Abraham might come on the Gentiles through Jesus Christ; that we might receive the promise of the Spirit through faith" (Gal. 3:14). The exercise of faith is always directed toward Christ. The experience of the Holy Spirit comes through experience with the risen Savior. It is "not a second experience independent of or in addition to Jesus Christ."[2]

1. The Spirit Generates New Life (Chapter 3:1-21)

The first direct reference John makes to the work of the Holy Spirit is taken from Jesus' conversation with Nicodemus. He said, "Ye must be born again." This refers to the work of the Spirit as the regenerative principle in human life. "Except a man be born of water and the Spirit, he cannot enter the kingdom of God."

The Spirit generates life in a rebirth. Nicodemus came to Jesus to discuss with Him issues pertaining to his religious experience. Jesus took him direct to the heart of such experience and told him that if he wants to see the kingdom of God he must be born again. At this point the man raised an intellectual problem without recognizing the prior need in his life, namely an experience with the Holy Spirit. Such a spiritual experience is the first necessity in the kingdom. There is no capacity in the natural man to discern spiritual truth. One must have a spiritual mind for that, one such as the Spirit alone can give to man.

The primary and essential source of the new birth is divine. It is the work of the Holy Spirit. A

191

spiritual life requires the effect of a spiritual operation. "We are his [God's] workmanship, created in Christ Jesus" (Eph. 2:10a). Notice again the relation of the Spirit's work to Christ. The spiritual life imparted to the individual believer is received upon confession of Jesus Christ. The Holy Spirit is the direct Agent involved in the transformation that takes place, but Christ is the Object of the saving faith. The spiritual birth is inseparably involved in a direct and personal faith in the Lord Jesus.

The Spirit generates power in rebirth. Natural generation has no capacity to transmit a spiritual nature. The power to overcome evil begins with a spiritual birth. The ability to perform the will of God comes from the Spirit's energizing work. "A spiritual nature, possessing spiritual capacities and born to a spiritual life, can only be generated by the Spirit."[3]

The ability and authority to involve the powers of heaven in the deadly conflict with evil reside in the Holy Spirit. He is the one who enables the believer to exercise the privileges of faith. He operates as the wind; the Spirit's voice can be heard in human utterances, His power can be felt in human actions, and His love can be expressed in human relationships. "To be born from above, to hear the voice of the Spirit, to know the mystery of His presence and working in the inner life are earthly things and not heavenly," in the sense of putting it off into some remote future.[4] These are spiritual realities that are open to all believers in Jesus Christ.

The Spirit generates hope in rebirth. Being born from above gives hope to enter heaven. He gives to believers a sense of the reality of their heavenly citizenship. The very real presence of the risen Christ is augmented by the very real hope of His return. This new life of the Spirit is eternal life. It has the quality of God's own life. Whosoever believes on the only begotten Son of God "shall not perish but have eternal life."

2. *The Spirit Sustains Eternal Life* (Chapter 3:31-36)

We are now referring to the last recorded testimony of John the Baptist. In his witness he refers to the fact that "a man can receive nothing, except it be given him from heaven." He insisted that Christ who came from heaven is above all. He asserts that anyone who receives the testimony of Christ "hath set to his seal that God is true."

God gave the Spirit to Christ without measure. This means that Christ in His humanity was given an unlimited supply of grace in the Spirit. God had no hesitation to impart the Spirit's wisdom and power with the fullness of divine assets. There was nothing lacking in His resources to meet the prevailing forces of evil. Christ made use of all that was available through the Spirit's presence. Throughout His life, living, serving, and witnessing in the power of the Spirit, Christ demonstrated that God is true to His promises. All who accept the witness of Jesus are thereby giving testimony that God is true. There is nothing lacking in the grace of God. "Jesus alone speaks without limit to His power to teach, since the spiritual life realizes itself in Him to the full measure of the Divine gift."[5]

Christ shares the Spirit without limit also. The grace of God, His gifts and power, are released

193

through His Son. The Spirit operates in conjunction with Christ and Christ operates through the Spirit. The Triune God, Father, Son, and Spirit, has a single goal and the three persons of the Godhead are one in purpose and action. The limitations are in man and not in God. When Christ opens the flow of influence from the Spirit, it is without restraint. The person having received Him determines the amount of grace to be received. The Spirit is available without limitation of grace. He gives gifts where He wills and to whom He wills, but the supply of wisdom needed to use the bestowed gifts is offered without discrimination.

The Christian believer has access to the Spirit without bounds. There is no reservation in the offer of God's free gift of grace. The "stops are all out" to share the full blast of heavenly music. The flow of divine blessings is full and the love and mercy of God are without measure. Man determines his own fullness by the extent of his openness and trust in God. He limits the flow of spiritual light and power by the quality of his own faith. The greatest fullness he knows is the possession of eternal life. This in itself opens the channels of grace and determines the nature of his spiritual experience.

3. *The Spirit Motivates Christian Worship*
(Chapter 4:1-26)

The familiar story of Jesus' casual meeting with the woman of Samaria has a wealth of meaning related to the Spirit's indwelling and His motivations to worship. This conversation with the Samaritan woman

194

opens deep insights about the believer's experience in the Spirit. He is not mentioned by name, but the inference is unmistakable. The living water of which Jesus speaks is the same inflow of new life mentioned in the conversation with Nicodemus. In this case we take another step in the doctrinal advance and see the result of life in the Spirit as an "overflow." The issue and the consummation of this new life is a spiritual dynamic that expresses itself in new dimensions. It produces an awareness of the riches in eternal life and creates a spiritual desire to worship God.

The concept of the Spirit life came from God. This is a revelation which became known through Jesus Christ. God is a spirit and therefore calls upon believers to offer up spiritual sacrifices. He is of Spirit essence. He is comprehended in terms of spiritual experience and divine illumination. God, who has revealed Himself in His Son, is known as the God of truth. He cannot be false and He cannot cancel out His promises. Our testimony sets the seal that "God is true." He is to be worshiped by those who recognize His essential worth. The spiritual worship which His Person deserves demands spiritual elements not found in the natural man. To worship God "in spirit and truth" is possible only through the Spirit of God. Reality in worship is achieved through experience of the Holy Spirit.

The reality of the Spirit life comes from Jesus Christ. This "water of life" is a gift from Him. It becomes in the believer a spiritual force that operates like an artesian well: it flows from an inner pressure. It is the overflow that makes the difference. Atti-

195

tudes toward others and relationships with them achieve a high level of understanding when prompted by the Spirit.

The Spirit's presence is a perennial spring beautifying the life with love and truth. It is a constant source of transforming power shaping the life to give glory to God.

The issue of this new life comes from the Spirit. Essentially His gift is eternal life. The life of the Spirit is integrated with the spirit of man. The believer is made capable of expressing high honors and deep adoration to God. The Spirit puts meaning into man's desire to worship. Without Him the forms of worship are hollow and lifeless.

Worship from the new life in Christ emanates from spiritual experience. True worship of God demands the expression of spiritual realities not found in the natural man. They rely upon the presence and power of the Holy Spirit to quicken from within and to prompt the soul expression of praise and thanksgiving.

4. The Spirit Provides Quickening Power (Chapter 6:53-65)

The teaching of this passage presupposes the work of the Holy Spirit. This "Bread of Life" discourse left many of the disciples in a serious dilemma. When Jesus said, "Except ye eat the flesh of the Son of man, and drink his blood, ye have no life in you," they were astonished. They could not understand how the offering of His flesh and blood as food and drink could give them eternal life. When Jesus had finished explaining the meaning of His remark, He added, "It is the spirit that quickeneth . . . the words that

I speak unto you, they are spirit and they are life." The disciples came to understand fully the "hard saying" after the outpouring of the Spirit on the day of Pentecost.

Spiritual response to Christ's pattern looks to Him for the true Way. As He lived by the pattern of the Father so He asks His disciples to live by the pattern of His own life. The quality of this life is divine and its nature is spiritual. As Christ lived by the Father so we live by Him.

When Jesus said, "I am the bread of life," He invited believers to make use of His life for their own. The source of eternal life is in Him, but the method of receiving it is through the Spirit. A spiritual response to the provision Christ made in giving Himself in death is finding the way to eternal life. On that basis the Spirit acts in transforming power to change the nature of the penitent soul. Then the believer grows in Christ as the Spirit of the Lord changes him continuously from one state of glory to another (2 Cor. 3:18). The dimensions of eternal life are measureless. Its consummation is a heavenly state. In the meantime the Spirit is at work adding more and more meaning to faith.

A spiritual response to Christ's promises enlarges the privileges of eternal life. "If any man eat of this bread, he shall live for ever." The perpetuation of eternal life rests upon a growing faith. Life in the Spirit is a perpetual growth. The fullness of that life relies upon obedience. The Holy Spirit is given "to those who obey him." Faith and obedience become the key to a growing spiritual life.

"On receiving Christ there should be no thirsting

197

after 'deeper' spiritual experiences as though the 'water' faith receives from Christ were not entirely satisfying or empowering."[6] It is important to avoid casting unfavorable reflection upon the "fulness of the blessing of the gospel of Christ" by demanding more than that offered through faith in Christ. This is basic to our understanding of the doctrine of the Holy Spirit.

5. *The Spirit Produces a Spiritual Overflow* (Chapter 7:37-39)

The Feast of the Tabernacles was on. People had gathered in Jerusalem at the close of the harvest to share with the crowds of Israel in a season of thanksgiving. The last day had a moving and dramatic ceremony. With the temple courts filled with people and the streets lined with spectators, the high priest engaged in a unique ritual. He took a silver pitcher from the temple and carried it joyously to the pool of Siloam. There he filled it with water (about two pints) and carried it back through the crowds to the temple. As he passed up the narrow lane formed by people on either side, the crowd chanted the promise God made to Israel through the prophet Isaiah: "With joy shall ye draw water out of the wells of salvation" (Is. 12:3). This forecast of the coming Messiah had in it a great hope for Israel. As the high priest entered the crowd-packed temple courts to perform the celebration, he carried the water around the altar seven times and then flung it on the altar of burnt offering as an offering to God. To the devout Israelite the symbolism was clear: (1) thanksgiving for water; (2) an acted prayer for rain; (3)

and a forecast of the days of their coming Messiah when God's people would draw water from the wells of salvation. They hoped for the day when God's Spirit would be poured out upon thirsty souls.

Imagine with me how Jesus must have stood there in the midst of the people waiting for the dramatic moment. While the dripping water wetted the ground about the altar, the voice of Jesus cried out between the temple walls, "If any man thirst, let him come unto me, and drink."

Coming to Christ introduces life in the Spirit. One who does will not only quench his own thirst for spiritual reality but also become a fountain of life to others. Not only is this water a source of spiritual grace unto life eternal, but it issues in a flow of influence for the benefit of others. Bear in mind that the comment about Jesus' announcement in the temple on the last day of the feast indicates that He had reference to the Holy Spirit. Any thirsty soul who comes to Jesus in faith believing shall be satisfied with the Spirit's gift of life eternal.

Believing in Christ sustains life in the Spirit. This involves the habitual practice of putting trust in Him for the saving effect of His death and resurrection. It means abiding in Him for His perpetual grace. The appropriation of Christ's work is essentially the act of opening the life for the Holy Spirit to come in. The individual believer becomes the "habitation of God through the Spirit." This concept of an abiding Presence is the chief characteristic of life in the Spirit.

Exalting Christ engages life in the Spirit. We make room for the Spirit's operation when we practice perpetual exaltation of Christ in our lives. It is essentially a matter of giving Him preeminence in every aspect of life. This is the chief purpose of the Spirit, to give Christ glory. As believers engage in the vocation of the Spirit, the manifestations of the Spirit become more and more evident. It is not that we seek more prominence of the Spirit, but rather that we give Christ the preeminence.

Faith in Jesus secures the gift of the Spirit. The faith is not in the Spirit but in Jesus. "For the reception of the Spirit, Jesus Christ is the sole, necessary object of faith." [7]

B. The Work of the Spirit in the Body of Believers

The second part of the Gospel of John speaks more specifically to the work of the Spirit in the corporate body of believers. This is particularly true of the upper room discourse. It contains the private instructions given to the disciples just before Christ's crucifixion and resurrection. Since they would soon be carrying the leadership responsibilities in the church, Jesus explained the coming and function of the Paraclete.

The word "Paraclete" should not be limited in its meaning to comfort in times of trouble or distress nor to consolation in time of sorrow. It includes these but conveys more. It means that He is one who puts courage into the believers. He empowers the church to cope with changing circumstances and demands and gives fortitude in the struggles of life. He makes the timid brave, gives wisdom to the faltering, and provides help in the difficult decisions of life. He does have enabling grace for the church to meet sorrows with resignation and to carry burdens with confidence. The predominant idea, however, is to put courage into the community of faith to meet the varying forces of opposition with resolution.

1. The Spirit Is a Perpetual Presence (Chapter 14:15-20)

"I will pray the Father, and he shall give you another Comforter."

The abiding presence of the Spirit is assured. The promise says, "the Father will give another Advocate." This is one in addition to the Lord Jesus. Christ is the Advocate interceding for the church at the right hand of God. The Spirit functions from within the church on earth. The Spirit lives and serves (abides) in the church. He fortifies its defense against adversaries. He supports the truth against error. He protects the fellowship of believers against darkness. He is now engaged in the work Christ began. The disciples had learned to know spiritual truth from Jesus, but later they came in direct contact with the Spirit.

The world cannot receive the Spirit. Its lack of spiritual sympathy disqualifies it from knowing Him. By "world" we mean that segment of society which refuses to accept the lordship of Christ. It is "human nature organizing itself without God." The company of the redeemed is in a position to receive the Spirit and to be a constant Presence in the midst. He makes real the presence of Christ and forms the pattern of group behavior.

When the Spirit's gracious presence is known in the church, the privileges of prayer are real. This awareness gives character to communion with the Father and adds the dimension of obedience. The Spirit is known to those who seek to do the will of God and to please the Lord Jesus. Obedience is a key to the Spirit's operation in the church. This attitude mingled with genuine love opens the way for Spirit contact. While the world can not know the Spirit, He is known to the church, which prays in the name of Christ, which obeys the teachings of Christ, and which loves the Father of Christ. In this context the Spirit can operate freely as an agent of courage and strength. This kind of life in the Spirit becomes the norm of the church.

When Christ left for heaven to enter into His mediatorial work, the Holy Spirit came into the church to carry on the promotion of the truth Christ revealed. The work of the One who said, "I am the truth," was given to the Spirit of Truth. Although He had dwelt with the disciples when Christ was in their midst, now the Spirit dwells in the church. This is a case of God's taking up permanent residence in the church by having the Spirit indwell the believers who know the truth and follow the Spirit of truth. In this corporate life in the Spirit the church realizes more and more "the perfect union of the Father and [the] Son and its own union with the Son through the Spirit in them and their life in Him."[8]

2. *The Spirit Is a Faithful Teacher* (Chapter 14:25, 26)

"The Comforter, which is the Holy Ghost, whom the Father will send in my name, he shall teach you all things."

The Spirit teaches in the name of Jesus. This is the way He was sent by the Father, "in the name of Jesus." In this sense the Spirit is presented to make the

Son known and to make His work intelligible to believers. He is carrying on the office of Jesus as the great Teacher. As Christ came in the name of His Father and not in His own name (Jn. 5:43), so the Spirit is here in the name of Jesus and finds His satisfaction in the glory of the Son. As a Teacher the Spirit is extending the ministry of Christ pointing to the joy of doing the will of the Father.

The Spirit teaches in complete understanding of the ways of God with man. All that belongs to the sphere of spiritual truth He illuminates and promotes in the church. "Nothing that is essential to the knowledge of God or to the guidance of life shall be wanting." The Spirit leads into the whole truth as a witness to the full expression of God's eternal purpose.

The Spirit teaches by bringing things to remembrance. His teaching follows the line of Christ's teaching. He enables the church to understand the meaning of what Christ taught. He illuminates what has been written about Christ and by Him. All that molds Christian belief and practice is included in the work of the Spirit. What Christ taught is basic to all that is given to the church in the subsequent teachings of the Spirit. Not all that God wants the church to know is recorded in the Gospels. The rest of the New Testament was inspired by the Spirit and holds an equal place of authority with the Gospels. It is clear, however, that nothing in the Acts and the Epistles holds any contradiction to what Christ taught.

The Spirit teaches what Christ taught. Basically there is nothing in the ministry of the Spirit that nullifies the teachings of Jesus. "As a teacher, the Paraclete would extend the scope of our Lord's earthly ministry without abandoning any part of the ground that Christ occupied."[9] It is precisely Christ's Word which is the truth. "If we let the Lord speak to us through His Word we shall distinguish with increasing clarity the general direction of His will and henceforth the Spirit will be able to guide us along that path in every detail of our daily life."[10]

3. *The Spirit Is an Effective Witness* (Chapter 15:26, 27)

"When the Comforter is come . . . he shall testify of me: and ye also shall bear witness."

The Spirit affirms the faith of believers. His ministry to the church centers in Christ. He is particularly concerned that Christ shall receive the honor due Him. The testimony about Jesus reveals the divine purpose to be accomplished in the Father's will. This is essentially a witness to the saving truth about Jesus. The Spirit is active in relating the needs of the soul to the redeeming love of the Savior. He also gives witness to the sustaining grace available through Christ. People need to know the assurance of faith. The Spirit's work in the church is a constant witness to the reality of the grace of God. The testimony about Jesus reveals the holy mission assigned to the church. The Spirit is the Director of missions and calls believers to dedicate their lives and skills to the witness of truth.

The Spirit uses the testimony of the believers. The testimony of the Spirit is given in the words, actions, and lives of people. In one sense He is the coordinating force in the life of the church. It takes Christian experience and divine unction combined to make an effective witness. Experience itself is ineffective. The Spirit does not supply lack of experience neither does experience supply a lack of unction. The Spirit brings both together to make Christ known. The collaboration of the human witness (experience) and the divine power (unction) is the norm for evangelism. The continuous joint testimony of Spirit and church makes the Christian witness effective.

4. *The Spirit Is a Convincing Reprover* (Chapter 16: 7-11)

> "When He [the Comforter] is come, he will reprove the world of sin, and of righteousness, and of judgment."

Conviction of the world is the work of the Spirit. When Jesus left, the invisible Spirit worked in the hearts of men to bring the claims of Christ to bear upon them. "Reprove" means both to convince and to convict. The Spirit convinces unto salvation and convicts unto condemnation. "The basic meaning of the word is so to demonstrate the truth to a man that he sees it as truth, that he is convinced of and admits his error, and that he accepts the new consequences which follow from the new acceptance of truth."[11]

The Spirit reproves the world with respect to sin. He detects and lays bare man's guilt and brings home to his conscience how sinful it is to refuse to believe on Jesus. He compels men to see that not to believe in Jesus Christ is sin. The primary mission of the Comforter to the unregenerate world is to convince them that the one damning sin is that of not believing in Christ.

The Spirit reproves the world in respect of righteousness. The earthly life of Jesus demonstrated the meaning of righteousness. He was completely conformed to the will of the Father. The Sinless One was tested by the severest suffering and triumphed in it. But the world remained unconvinced even by the cross. The one perfect model of human righteousness was rejected. But now the Spirit functions to convince men of the supreme goodness and greatness of Jesus. He convinces the sinful world that righteousness is now available and adequate. There was no way to achieve righteousness until Christ made provision for it. The Spirit is active in helping men see this provision and to realize their need for it.

The Spirit reproves the world in respect of judgment. A crisis is at hand! There is no way to avoid responsibility for our decisions. We cannot escape the consequence of our choices. At the end every man stands before the Eternal Judge.

Judgment began with the cross. There what appeared to be a defeat was turned into victory. The ruler of this world was judged. Satan was given a death blow because atonement was made for sin. The Spirit brings this fact home to the minds of men. The resurrection following the crucifixion of Jesus was the final evidence that Satan is defeated. Judgment in the end lies with God to be executed by Jesus Christ.

The world must be convinced that God's saving action in Christ has accomplished the redemptive purpose. "The awakening to sin, the realization of judgment, the discovery of Christ, the assurance of salvation are all the work of the Holy Spirit of God."[12] This function of the Spirit is to bring to the world "the conviction that there is such a thing as sin, that the essence of sin is refusal to believe in Christ; that there is such a thing as righteousness, and that it is embodied in the incarnate Christ and attested by His return to heaven; that there is such a thing as judgment, and that judgment consists in the triumph over sin, through Christ's righteousness. It is a conviction of man's guilt in rejecting Christ, Christ's righteousness and acceptance by the Father, and His final victory over Satan."[13]

5. *The Spirit Is a Reliable Guide* (Chapter 16:12-15)

> "When he, the Spirit of truth, is come, he will guide you into all truth . . . he will shew you things to come."

Jesus had many things yet to say. He could not tell everything to the disciples. They did not yet have the capacity to support the burden of fuller teachings. He would teach more later through the Holy Spirit.

The Spirit does not speak from Himself. He declares what He hears; He is an unfolder of truth, giving witness to its meaning.

He is engaged in glorifying Christ. He discloses the essential character of Jesus and declares the significance of His work. He brings to light the nature of Christ's excellence but does not add to His glory.

The revelation of God is completed by the coming of the Spirit. The provisions for redemption are all made. Now it is the work of the Spirit to perform the function of a Guide to direct the church in its learning and understanding of the will of God.

The Spirit shows things to come. The believer rests in the assurance that whatever the future holds for him there is One committed to be with him. He relies on the Spirit to see consequences ahead of any course of action that might be chosen.

The declaration of things to come involves a broad view of the growing church. The Spirit was delegated to carry forward the teachings of Christ and apply them to the new community of faith. He was to enlighten the believers "of that great and untried life which was about to open before the church at Pentecost and to reach its perfection at the second coming."[14]

The Spirit was engaged through the centuries since Pentecost in fulfilling this function. It is truly the dispensation of the Spirit. Read the Book of Acts and see how active He was in the shaping of church life, in planning strategy, in facing opposition, in formulating policies, and in using the Word. He was engaged in the whole process of unfolding truth and in setting the pattern of apostolic practices.

The Christian today is in constant need for direction in his work, witness, and worship. He relies upon the Spirit for grace and power to live for Christ. He often sings:

"Holy Spirit, faithful Guide,
Ever near the Christian's side,
Gently lead us by the hand,
Pilgrims in a desert land."

Conclusion

After the resurrection Jesus appeared with the closeted disciples and addressed them with, "Peace be unto you," followed by the command to take the Holy Spirit with them. He gave them this great blessing with the view to endow them with a vital force for holy living and Christian service. The remitting and retaining of sins having been delegated to the church calls for the constant work of the Holy Spirit.

It is to be observed that there is nothing said in the Gospel of John about the gifts of the Spirit. He has laid the foundation truth about the Spirit with doctrine. He speaks about the reality of the Spirit and the believer's intimate relationship with Him. Those who formulate their views of the Holy Spirit on Bible doctrine use these basic truths as the primary source of understanding.

The Spirit is involved in transformation, spiritual worship, Christian witness, and magnifying Jesus Christ. In the church He engages the body of believers in direct conflict with the forces of evil, in promoting the teachings of Christ, in bearing witness to the truth, in confronting the world with the claims of the gospel, and in glorifying Christ. The primary concern is to exalt Jesus Christ and to establish assurance of eternal life.

1. William Barclay, *The Promise of the Spirit* (Westminster; 1960), p. 30.

2. Frederick Dale Bruner, *A Theology of the Holy Spirit*, p. 227.

3. Henry Barclay Swete, *The Holy Spirit in the New Testament* (Macmillan; 1910), p. 133.

4. *Ibid.*, p. 135.

5. *Ibid.*, p. 137.

6. Bruner, *op. cit.*, p. 254.

7. *Ibid.*, p. 254.

8. Swete, *op. cit.*, p. 152.

9. *Ibid.*, p. 153.

10. Rene Pache, *The Person and Work of the Holy Spirit* (Moody; 1954), p. 153.

11. Barclay, *op cit.*, p. 43.

12. Barclay, *op. cit.*, p. 45.

13. J. Oswald Sanders, *The Holy Spirit of Promise* (Marshall, Morgan and Scott; 1940), p. 47.

14. Swete, *op. cit.*, p. 163.

13

THE INCARNATIONAL WORK OF THE HOLY SPIRIT

By Richard C. Detweiler

This discussion is to be confined to the Synoptics (Mark, Luke, and Matthew), not including John. I would remind us that even these earlier three Gospels were written well after Pentecost, later than some of Paul's letters, and in the context of the early church. Therefore, we should not think the Synoptic Gospels represent an understanding of the Holy Spirit that is ignorant of His activity beyond the resurrection and the ascension. It is true that in the Synoptics the references to the Spirit are present more in the background than in the foreground and do not afford the more complete picture of the person and work of the Spirit given us by John and in Paul's letters, but the Synoptics are not an inferior revelation of the doctrine of the Spirit, especially when we remember that Luke-Acts is a combined work.

A second observation has to do with the background of the Gospels with regard to the Holy Spirit. We may ask why references to the Spirit in the first three Gospels are not numerous. The words recorded as *spoken by Jesus* contain only seven references to the Spirit, if we do not count parallel references more than once in the three Gospels.

In the words of the Synoptic writers *about Jesus*, more references to the Holy Spirit are found. But even here they are not abundant and they appear almost entirely at the beginning of the record in regard to Jesus' birth, baptism, temptation, and the commencement of His ministry.[1]

We may already glean our first lessons from the Synoptic scarcity of reference to the Holy Spirit. It was clear to all that Jesus had received the fullness of the Spirit without measure in His incarnate life. But Jesus sensed His own relation with the Father with such immediacy or closeness that there was less need for Him or for others near Him to speak of the Spirit as a mediating agent. The Spirit's work was seen in and through Christ (incarnational work) rather than running parallel to Christ, and it was constant rather than periodic. In the Old Testament the Spirit moved alongside the servants of God and at times fell on them for greater or lesser periods to fulfill certain functions or offices which required the activity of the Spirit.

In the incarnation of Christ, the Spirit was joined in continuous oneness with a particular life in the world, the perfect servant, of whom Isaiah says: "The Spirit of the Lord shall *rest* upon him" (Is.

11:2). This continuous oneness with Christ marked a new stage of the Spirit's operation in the world and was different in manifestation. Deeds now issued out of a life in the Spirit, not from a periodic "falling upon."

Jesus was the very bearer of the Spirit into the new age. Therefore He did not express His infilling of the Spirit in the ecstatic ways that characterized the anointings and prophesyings of the Old Testament and which gave prominence to the Spirit Himself as He came upon judges, kings, prophets, and others. As the continuous bearer of the Spirit, Jesus' Spirit-fullness reflected the deeper rootage of an uninterrupted fellowship with the Father characterized by perfect oneness and obedience which is the complete incarnational work of the Spirit. That does not exclude the ecstatic element from the Holy Spirit's manifestation in the New Testament age, but it subordinates the ecstatic manifestations of the Spirit to His incarnational work of creating a fullness of life in relation with God. For example, the phenomenon of glossolalia indicates both the infilling of the Spirit and at the same time is a reminder that the ultimate experience of the Spirit as reflected in Christ is beyond ecstasy in a continuous oneness of life with God. The new work of the Spirit as introduced by the Gospels is His incarnational work. The transition from the Old Testament brought by Jesus was from the manifestation of the Spirit primarily in deeds to His manifestation in life out of which deeds flowed. This is our first major point of reference for understanding the New Testament doctrine of the Spirit.

It has been said that the incarnational work of the

Spirit is His major work since the purpose of the Spirit is to make Christ known. The full scope of that incarnational work now leads us to focus on three of its aspects: (1) The Holy Spirit and the Incarnate Birth, (2) The Holy Spirit and the Incarnate Life, and (3) The Holy Spirit and the Incarnate Death, Resurrection, and Glorification.

1. The Holy Spirit and the Incarnate Birth

The incarnation of Christ reveals that the Holy Spirit is divine person. Let us note the Luke 1:34, 35 and Matthew 1:20 passages.

Luke and Matthew emphasize along with the virgin birth, and even more so, that the incarnation of the Son of God was accomplished through the activity of the Holy Spirit. We rightly affirm that this supports the divinity of Christ, but we should remember inversely that the work of incarnation also affirms the divine personal character of the Holy Spirit as the agent of incarnation. If Jesus is acknowledged as divine, it follows that only divinity could accomplish the incarnation of divinity. Furthermore, the incarnation of God in a particular man is not the pantheistic incarnation of non-Christian religions, but personalistic; so then again the incarnational work of the Spirit certifies Him not only as divine but as divine *person*, not an impersonal, pantheistic force.

To accept the divine-human incarnation of the Son of God requires that we acknowledge the agent of the incarnation as divine and personal. In fact, the two great signs that the Holy Spirit is personal God are His works of incarnation and resurrection. Here we already part company with the theology of Jehovah's Witnesses, Unitarians, Jesus Only, and other semi-Christian groups along with non-Christian religions which see the Spirit as impersonal power emanating from God and therefore something less than divine in itself.

The personal involvement of the Holy Spirit with the incarnation has two further implications. First, since the Spirit's incarnational work verifies Him as divine person, it also affirms the triune nature of the Godhead. As Georgia Harkness says, "The doctrine of the Trinity [if we can refer to it as a 'doctrine'] rests centrally on the incarnation."[2] If the incarnation of the Son requires us to deal with the reality of the Holy Spirit, and likewise with the Father, we have already the implied Trinity. That is why anti-Trinitarian theology has to start with denying the deity of the incarnation and the personal agent thereof.

Second, the incarnation introduces the unique relation of the Spirit to Christ. In the Synoptic Gospels the Spirit is not seen apart from Jesus. This is our second major point of reference. We have been searching for some theological North Star to fix our bearings on the person and work of the Spirit. If we resolve the relation of the Spirit to Christ, we have the measure by which the Spirit and His work are most consistently understood throughout the New Testament. The Holy Spirit is revealed exclusively in the Synoptics as the Spirit of Christ, and primarily so in the rest of the New Testament. This leads us to our next portion of study, namely, the Holy Spirit and the incarnate life.

2. The Holy Spirit and the Incarnate Life

The Holy Spirit's incarnational work began with the conception and birth of Christ. But the incarnation extends into the incarnate life of our Lord. The Word that was made flesh dwelt among us. The incarnation is co-extensive with the whole life and ministry of Christ, not merely His entrance upon it at the Nativity.[3]

The incarnational work of the Holy Spirit was manifest during Jesus' life in three major events.

The first was Jesus' baptism, recorded in all three Synoptics. Let's look at the Luke passage, beginning with Luke 3:15. The question is whether Jesus is the Christ. Luke supplies a threefold answer. First, Luke records John the Baptist's answer: "He will baptize you with the Holy Spirit and with fire" (3:16). Only the anointed Messiah as the bearer of the Spirit could baptize with the Spirit. Second, is the confirmation (the dove) that Jesus had indeed received the Spirit (3:22). And third, the ultimate purpose of the baptism is the confirmation of Jesus' sonship by the Father (3:22).

Now turning to Matthew 3:15 we have Jesus' own statement that His baptism was in order to fulfill all righteousness. That means it was to confirm His right and full relation with God which was brought about and maintained by the work of the Holy Spirit and which qualified Him for His ministry. This is the key to understanding the meaning of Jesus' baptizing with the Spirit. As He Himself was baptized by the Spirit as the manifestation of His full relation with the Father, so likewise Jesus' baptizing with the Spirit was to complete the relation of believers with Himself. This would qualify them to be His witnesses even as He by the Spirit bore witness out of His oneness with the Father.

In other words, Jesus' ministry was always dependent on His oneness of relation with the Father as the incarnate Son, and this relation was dependent on the continued incarnational work of the Spirit, not on Jesus' status as one of the Godhead.

From the Synoptics' standpoint by implications the baptism of the Holy Spirit by Jesus would have to do primarily with establishing believers in a full relationship with God through union with Christ. The baptism of the Spirit is the baptism of the believer into the incarnate life of Christ which is expressed most fully as Christ's body, the church.

The continued incarnational work of the Spirit becomes further clear in the event of Jesus' temptation into which the Spirit led Him. The power of Jesus in the temptation did not lie in His divinity, but in the perfection of His incarnate life, His complete obedience to the Father, which was not legalistic but grew out of His constant fullness of relation with the Father made possible by the continued work of the Spirit in Him. The temptations were attacks not against His divinity but to overthrow His incarnate life, and His victory was in the Spirit. In His incarnate life, Jesus lived out our life for us in the power of the Spirit. The work of the Spirit is now to make Jesus' victorious life (as well as His death) available to us. The power of the Spirit is the power of the incarnate life of Christ made operative in us by the Holy Spirit.

The third event revealing the Spirit's work in Jesus' life is the continuous event of His ministry. Two passages may be noted: Luke 4:18 and Matthew 12:28. I would make only one point here. The power of Jesus' ministry was the fruit of the Spirit. We should caution ourselves not to distinguish too sharply between the fruit and the gifts of the Spirit. The fruit of the Spirit was and is the incarnate life of Christ — *then* the life of Jesus, *now* His life in us. The gifts of the Spirit are the operations or the functioning of the life in Christ. Jesus' ministry was the *active outworking of His incarnate life in the Spirit.* The gifts of the Spirit cannot be separated from the fruit of the transformed life which in Jesus was fully manifest, for He was without sin. One more Scripture might be noted, Matthew 12:31. This refers to blasphemy against the Holy Spirit and is recorded in all three Synoptics. Matthew and Mark both put the issue into the context of Jesus' ministry. Jesus says in effect that when His ministry is regarded as not being of the Spirit, the credibility of His life is undercut and the offending person thereby cuts himself off from the activity of God. So even the matter of blasphemy against the Spirit has to do not with the Spirit alone, but with regard to acceptance or rejection of the ministry the Spirit performs through the incarnate Son.

Finally, we move a shade beyond the Synoptic scope of this subject for a final comment on the work of the Spirit in the incarnate death, resurrection, and glorification of Christ.

217

3. *The Holy Spirit and the Incarnate Death, Resurrection, and Glorification*

The Synoptics do not speak of the Spirit in connection with these aspects of Christ's incarnate being. We are indebted to other Scriptures such as Hebrews 9:14, which records that Christ through the eternal Spirit offered Himself without spot to God. And the words of Paul that it was the Spirit who effected the resurrection of Christ.

The important point I want to make is that the incarnational work of the Holy Spirit extends not only throughout the span of Jesus' human existence on earth but continues in His glorified humanity today. It is through the continuation of the incarnate life of Christ today that the Spirit joins believers with Him. We are members of His body, of His flesh and of His bones, is one way of saying it. In other words, we are not joined to a Spirit Jesus, but to an incarnate Christ by the Spirit.

The next stage in the renewal of emphasis on the Spirit today and on the "now Jesus" or the "Spirit Jesus" will be the resurgence of mysticism. "Jesus" will become a kind of occultic password into the mystical world rather than the incarnate center of faith and relation with a personal God. The fruit of the Spirit is then seen primarily in terms of mystical experience rather than transformed ethical life and character. The gifts of the Spirit then become confused with magical powers and spiritual forces afloat in the universe. Prayer becomes plugging into spiritual currents available to mystical faith, healing is likewise viewed, and tongues become spiritistic incantations. In fact, the forces of Anti-Christ will more likely be in spiritistic form than atheistic, and will be marked by mystical powers which will set themselves up as God and perform miraculous wonders. This can be overcome only insofar as the activity of the Spirit is held together with a personal faith-relationship with the incarnate Christ.

One of the challenges today is discernment of the spirits. This is why the norm of the person and work of the Spirit is His relation to the incarnate Christ (1 Jn. 4:1-3). The purpose of Christ's incarnation was to make union with His life available to us. The reason Jesus said the Spirit could not come until He Himself had gone away is that Jesus' exaltation and glorification had to be accomplished before the Spirit could apply the completed work. The Spirit's incarnational work could not be mediated to believers until it was complete in the glorification of Jesus' humanity. The goal of Christ's redemptive activity is to bring redeemed men not into rarefied mystical experience but into Christ's resurrected and glorified manhood. The putting on of the new man which is created in righteousness and true holiness is the extension of the incarnational work of the Spirit. As Newbigin states it in *The Household of God,* "it was by the Holy Spirit that the Word took flesh of the Virgin Mary. It is by the Holy Spirit that He has now a new body, a body into which only the Holy Spirit can engraft us."

The presence of the Spirit does not supersede the presence of Christ. It is centered in the incarnate, glorified Christ. The Christian experience of the Holy Spirit has as its content the encounter with the living Christ. This is the basic lesson begun for us in the Synoptic Gospels and unfolded throughout the New Testament — "Christ in you the hope of glory" (Col. 1:27).

That theme is to be continued in our witness and ministry of the gospel, and gives meaning to Jesus' words, "Baptizing them in the name of the Father, and of the Son, and of the Holy Ghost" (Mt. 28:19).

Bibliography

Berkhof, Hendrikus, "The Doctrine of the Holy Spirit" (John Knox, 1964)

Harkness, Georgia, "The Fellowship of the Holy Spirit" (Abingdon, 1966)

Hendry, George S., "The Gospel of the Incarnation" (Westminster, 1958)

————, "The Holy Spirit in Christian Theology" (Westminster, 1956)

1. See Georgia Harkness, "The Doctrine of the Holy Spirit."
2. Ibid., p. 103.
3. George S. Hendry, "The Gospel of the Incarnation," p. 95.

14

THE
HOLY SPIRIT
AND
PRAYER

Introduction

By Paul G. Landis

Prayer is more than a combination of trite memorized phrases rearranged to fit the occasion which must at times sound silly to God. What is true prayer? Perhaps the following definitions will be helpful:

"What the church needs today is not more machinery or better, not new organizations or more and novel methods *but* men whom the Holy Ghost can use. Men of prayer. Men mighty in prayer. Men are God's method. The church is looking for better methods; God is looking for better men. The Holy Ghost does not flow through methods but through men. He does not come on machinery but on men. He does not anoint plans but men — men of prayer" (E. M. Bounds in *Power Through Prayer*).

"The highest form of communion is not asking God

221

for things for ourselves but letting Him flow down through us out over the world — in endless benediction" (Frank Laubach in *Prayer the Mightiest Force in the World*).

"To pray is to let Jesus into our hearts. Our prayers are always a result of Jesus knocking at our heart's door. All He needs is access and He enters in wherever He is not denied admittance. To pray is nothing more involved than to open the door giving Jesus access to our needs and permitting Him to exercise His own power in dealing with them. Prayer is an attitude of our hearts toward God. An attitude which He in heaven immediately recognizes as prayer, as an appeal to His heart" (O. Hallesby in his book *Prayer*).

"[Prayer] is not merely a flash of Godward desire, but the passionate fervor of a whole self that pants to know God and His will above all other knowing. It is not a hurried visit to the window of a religious drive-in restaurant for a moral sandwich or a cup of spiritual stimulant, but an unhurried communion with God who is never in a hurry. It is not merely the expression of a transient mood of dependence or loneliness, but the consistent cry of one who seeks to perceive and express the Ultimate Beauty. It is the antithesis of dilly-dally devotions, drowsy murmurs from a pillow where sleep lies in wait, the lazy lisping of familiar phrases that should shake one to the core of one's being. It is the find-or-die outreach of the soul for God" (Albert Edward Day in *Existence Under God*).

We sing "Prayer is the soul's sincere desire uttered or unexpressed." It is that which we really want from the bottom of our heart. "Delight thyself also in the Lord; and he shall give thee the desires of thine heart" (Ps. 37:4).

A. *Prayer and the Coming of the Holy Spirit*

In the New Testament prayer is always associated with the coming of the Holy Spirit to a group or individuals. Jesus commanded His disciples to wait; not to leave Jerusalem nor to enter into their task. They were to wait for the coming of the Spirit. We need always to recognize that we cannot do the work of Jesus without His Spirit.

So they waited, how? With *prayer and supplication* (Acts 1:14). God cannot speak to us unless by listening we give Him a chance to speak. He cannot give His gifts, especially the gift of His Spirit, unless we open ourselves to these gifts.

That is what *real* prayer does, if it is "the passionate fervor of a whole self that pants to know God and His will above all other knowing."

Notice the following Scriptures:

> Isaiah 55:6 — "Seek ye the Lord while he may be found, call ye upon him while he is near."
> Psalm 145:18 — "The Lord is nigh unto all them that call upon him, to all that call upon him in truth."
> James 4:8 — "Draw nigh to God, and he will draw nigh to you."
> Acts 4:31 — "When they had prayed, the place was shaken where they were assembled together; and they were all filled with the Holy Ghost, and they spake the word of God with boldness."

When they had prayed. So often we move about, so

empty, with God seeming so far away. In prayer we could simply come, seek, and find, ask and receive. As we communicate with God, His Spirit can flow, fill, and empower as we wait, as we pray, and as we receive by faith. The Holy Spirit will not force Himself upon anyone who does not ask in prayer. Jesus said: "Ask, and it shall be given you; seek, and ye shall find; knock, and it shall be opened unto you: for every one that asketh receiveth; and he that seeketh findeth; and to him that knocketh it shall be opened. Or what man is there of you, whom if his son ask bread, will he give him a stone? Or if he ask a fish, will he give him a serpent?" "If ye then, being evil, know how to give good gifts unto your children, *how much more* shall your heavenly Father give the Holy Spirit to them that ask him" (Mt. 7:7-10 and Lk. 11:13)?

Jesus said to the woman at the well: "If thou knewest the gift of God, and who it is that saith to thee, Give me to drink; thou wouldest have asked of him and he would have given thee living water. . . . But whosoever drinketh of the water that I shall give him shall never thirst; but the water that I shall give him shall be *in him* a well of water springing up into everlasting life" (Jn. 4:10, 14).

Jesus is offering living water, a well within us springing up into everlasting life. In prayer we must ask to receive. Jesus promised that "Whatsoever ye shall ask the Father in my name, he will give it you. . . . Ask, and ye shall receive, that your joy may be full. . . . For the Father himself loveth you" (Jn. 16:23, 24, 27).

Do we really believe these words of Jesus enough to

ask in simple faith? Dare we ask from God all that He wants to give us through our having access to Him through prayer? We can ask, we can receive, and our joy can be full! Prayer and fasting often go together as we bring all our senses under His control, and as we praise, worship, and adore Him. Fasting and prayer must be unto the Lord and not for selfish motives, as Jesus warned so well in Matthew 6:16-18. We must not let gifts, enduements of power, and answers to prayer become more important than worshiping or seeking the Giver.

B. What Is the Place of the Holy Spirit in Our Prayers?

True worship of God must be in the Spirit. Where the Spirit is *absent* all forms of worship are empty and meaningless. Where the Spirit is *present*, men know that they are in the presence of God. " . . . be filled with the Spirit. Speak to one another in the words of psalms, hymns, and sacred songs; sing hymns and psalms to the Lord, with praise in your hearts. Always give thanks for everything to God the Father, in the name of our Lord Jesus Christ" (Eph. 5:18-20, *Today's English Version*).

Do we allow the Holy Spirit to control our personal prayer life and our congregational prayers and worship? God through His Spirit anticipates our prayers. He said, "I will answer them before they even call to me: while they are still talking to me about their needs I will go ahead and answer their prayers" (Is. 65:24, *Living Bible*).

We do not need to remain prayerless or weak in our prayers, for the Holy Spirit assists us in our prayers.

"So too the Spirit assists us in our weakness; for we do not know how to pray aright; but the Spirit pleads for us with sighs that are beyond words; and He who searches the human heart knows what is in the mind of the Spirit, since the Spirit pleads before God for the saints" (Rom. 8:26, 27, Moffatt).

C. H. Dodd has said, "By ourselves we cannot pray aright, because we do not know what to ask for. We do not know what to ask for, because we cannot see a day or even an hour ahead, and because even in any given situation we do not know what is best for us."

In a recent time of disappointment and grief my wife said, "It seems that someone else has to word the prayers for us."

"Prayer is the divine in us appealing to God above us. All we can do is bring to God an inarticulate sigh of appeal and the Holy Spirit will translate that sigh of ours to God. Here is the noblest of all conceptions of the Spirit. We *must* pray. We do not know for what to pray, all we can do is to take to God the desperate voiceless longing of the human heart, the inarticulate, wordless sigh; and when that happens, the Spirit is there to take our prayer and to place it before God as it ought to be prayed. The Spirit is the interpreter of the prayers of men. It is the wonder of the Spirit that the Spirit not only brings God to men but also brings men to God. So often in prayer all words seem inadequate; so often, when life is at its most bewildering and its most wounding and heart-breaking, there is nothing but a dumb longing for God. That is prayer at its highest; and that is when the Spirit breaks in and interprets and translates our
226

prayer to God" (William Barclay in *The Promise of the Spirit*, p. 86).

It is the work of the Holy Spirit to bring us as brethren together in our small group relationships or in our larger congregations. Jesus promised that when we gather together or even when two of us agree on anything, then His presence is right there among us. When brother and brother come together in reconciliation and correction, there Jesus by His Spirit is in their midst. Only the Holy Spirit can bring about the miracle of reconciliation by bringing two who have been separated by unlove to forgivensss, to love, and to surrender at the foot of the cross.

There is no place in the life of the Spirit or in our prayers in the Spirit for individualism which strikes down and disregards the voice of our brothers and sisters for "through him we both have access by one Spirit unto the Father" (Eph. 2:18).

"Confess your faults one to another, and pray one for another, that ye may be healed" (Jas. 5:16).

I believe that we abide in Christ and He abides in us through the Holy Spirit's presence in Jesus.

The Holy Spirit will continue to indwell and fill, only as we repent of all sin, hindrances, and lack of commitment that enter our life. No matter how great our experiences of baptisms, infillings, or anointings, the only way to walk in the Spirit is to repent and be cleansed of any and all known sin. Colossians 4:6 — "As ye have therefore received Christ Jesus the Lord, so walk ye in him."

Jesus promised that if we abide in Him and He in us we can ask what we will and it will be done unto us. This relationship through the Holy Spirit gives us the channel of prayer and the courage to ask for our deepest personal needs.

> "But if any of you lacks wisdom, he should pray to God, who will give it to him; for God gives generously and graciously to all. But you must believe when you pray, and not doubt at all; for whoever doubts is like a wave in the sea that is driven and blown about by the wind. Any such person must not think that he will receive anything from the Lord" (Jas. 1:5-7, *Today's English Version*).

> "Yea, if thou criest after knowledge, and liftest up thy voice for understanding, . . . then shalt thou understand the fear of the Lord, and find the knowledge of God" (Prov. 2:3, 5).

C. *Prayer in the Holy Spirit*

> "But you, my friends, keep on building yourselves up in your most sacred faith. Pray *in* the power of the Holy Spirit" (Jude 20, TEV).

Prayer can be a very selfish activity. It can be merely seeking to use God for one's own purposes. As we pray *in* the Spirit, then we honestly pray "thy will be done" and not, "thy will be changed." Prayer is not only asking God but allowing God to ask us. Praying in the Spirit is allowing the Spirit to control our thoughts and our concerns.

A member of the youth group recently shared that she has been praying for my wife and me for several weeks. And she was praying *in* the Spirit, He revealed to her some needs that no one else had communicated to her. The Spirit used her to minister deeply to us in our needs.

228

"Praying always with all prayer and supplication *in the Spirit,* and watching thereunto with all perseverance and supplication for all saints" (Eph. 6:18).

This is a level of prayer that most of us do not experience enough. As we pray in the Spirit our concerns and thoughts go beyond ourselves to the needs of others.

In 1 Corinthians 14:14, 15, Paul gives some insight on praying in the Spirit.

"For if I pray in an unknown tongue, my spirit prayeth, but my understanding is unfruitful.

"What is it then? I will pray with the spirit, and I will pray with the understanding also: I will sing with the spirit, and I will sing with the understanding also."

Praying in supplication, with requests, and in praise can be controlled by the Spirit and these go beyond our own intellectual understanding of what He is saying and doing through our prayers.

"I am the Lord thy God, which brought thee out of the land of Egypt: open thy mouth wide, and I will fill it" (Ps. 81:10).

I believe there are times when the Lord just wants us to praise and adore Him and open our mouths and let His Holy Spirit fill them with praise and requests in prayer.

Conclusion

I believe that the words of Jesus to the church today would be: I want men everywhere and always to pray and not to lose heart. (Compare Luke 18:1). Prayer doesn't change things, God does, and that makes prayer all the greater. Can we honestly share in worship with David?

"I love the Lord, because he hath heard my voice and my supplications. Because he hath inclined his ear unto me, therefore will I call upon him as long as I live" (Ps. 116:1, 2).

15

THE
HOLY SPIRIT
AND
EVANGELISM

By Myron S. Augsburger

Therefore seeing we have this ministry, as we have received mercy, we faint not;

But have renounced the hidden things of dishonesty, not walking in craftiness, nor handling the word of God deceitfully; but by manifestation of the truth commending ourselves to every man's conscience in the sight of God.

But if our gospel be hid, it is hid to them that are lost:

In whom the god of this world hath blinded the minds of them which believe not, lest the light of the glorious gospel of Christ, who is the image of God, should shine unto them.

For we preach not ourselves, but Christ Jesus the Lord; and ourselves your servants for Jesus' sake.

For God, who commanded the light to shine out of darkness, hath shined in our hearts, to give the light of the knowledge of the glory of God in the face of Jesus Christ.

But we have this treasure in earthen vessels, that the excellency of the power may be of God, and not of us.

— 2 Cor. 4:1-7

The Anabaptists were the Christian existentialists of the sixteenth century. They spoke from an experience with the risen Christ, and baptized believers as a sign that they were sharing the resurrection life. This was a unique emphasis in sixteenth-century Christianity.

Born in Zurich, 1525, under the evangelical preaching of Zwingli, the Anabaptists took his message seriously, "It is not the outward baptism with water which saves a man, but the inner baptism with the Spirit." Hundreds of years before the rise of Pentecostalism they had both a personal experience with the Holy Spirit and a theology of the Spirit. They regarded the experience of being a new creature, living in the Spirit, as basic for the believer's church and for the witness of the kingdom.

A similar uniqueness was their involvement in evangelism. While the other major Christian groups regarded the Commission of Christ (Mt. 28:19, 20) to have been only for the first century, the Anabaptists took it as a continuing mandate. They evangelized with such intensity across Europe that Roland Bainton says: "Both Lutherans and Catholics were afraid that all of Europe would become Anabaptist."

This is our heritage, a spiritual and evangelistic brotherhood. The church has a commitment to biblicism and to discipleship. Consequently there are four marks of the church, and they are essential to our denomination's life: internally, they are (1) conversion, (2) a disciplined brotherhood, and externally, (3) freedom from the powers of the state and (4) evangelistic witness. The Holy Spirit helps us keep these in balance.

Evangelism is a call to commitment, both within the congregation and beyond. Within the congregation of believers evangelism functions in Christian nurture, leading our youth to an understanding and commitment to Christ. Evangelism beyond the church is witnessing with the intent of persuasion (2 Cor. 5:11); it is making faith in Christ a clear option so that men can believe (2 Cor. 4:6).

There are three primary functions to evangelism: communication, compassion, and calling to commitment. In communication we are presenting the kerygma, the good news of the gospel. In compassion we are sharing the love of Christ in a way which understands and cares for the person being won to Christ. In the call to commitment there must be honesty and fairness to the person being invited to Christ. We should remember that God never violates the human personality. This means that we who work in the various forms of evangelism avoid gimmicks, never misuse people.

Perhaps you have observed, as others of us have,

patterns where men use "trick steps" in giving their invitation at the close of a message. Or where more sensational persons claim gifts from the Spirit to call out problems in the audience and get persons to respond, claiming by this performance to convince them that God is at work among them. The open style of Billy Graham, to preach and simply give an invitation, may be a far greater evidence of trusting the Spirit to convince men of Christ.

It is the Holy Spirit who is actually God's Evangelist; at best we are only tools. When He gives the church the gift of an evangelist it is the Spirit who uses the man to call persons to Christ. Let us look now at how the Spirit works through men in evengelism.

I. The Holy Spirit Prepares the Witness

Christ baptizes with the Spirit, and does so when we surrender to Him as Lord. In the new birth, or experience of regeneration, one's own spirit is made alive or brought into a living relation with God. But in addition to what the Spirit of Christ does in making the believer's spirit alive unto God (sharing the resurrection), Christ baptizes with His Spirit, and His Spirit is another Spirit in addition to our spirit. From this relationship we then speak of the indwelling of the Spirit, and the further filling of the Spirit. By His presence the Holy Spirit prepares us to witness for Christ, granting us assurance of salvation, or assurance that we are in Christ. One will never be an effective witness until he is certain of his own relation to the Lord.

It is His presence and power which leads us to victory in our personal lives. By His work with us we participate in the therapy of honesty. We discover the inauthentic facets of our personality and allow Him to help us work through them to become authentic persons. He releases us from perversions that are there as our attempt to escape something, our insecurity, our attempt to prove something, or simply our pride and ego struggle. He provides a sense of belonging, of being at ease with one's self in grace, so that we can live in freedom and victory, with a good self-image and a Christ-controlled ego. Our witness can then be fair and honest, as we confront others with Christ.

Another work of the Spirit is to give us discernment in the Word. This gift, to understand the spirit of Scripture and to discover its prophetic implication, is essential for effective witness. The gift of prophecy is the gift to "forth-tell" a word from the Lord. This word becomes, as Donald Miller says in his book on *Biblical Preaching,* "the biblical meaning or word happening again."

The Spirit also gives unction or anointing for effective communication. John writes that "ye have an unction from the Holy One, and ye know all [spiritual] things." He guides us with wisdom in our selection of content and anoints us with wisdom to understand those to whom we are witnessing. This understanding of God's message for a particular person's need is the Spirit's function within us.

Another very important aspect of His work in us is creating the freedom to empathize. One of our greater needs in Christian work is compassion. This comes in part from sharing with people in need, but it is the love of the Spirit through us which keeps us from mere pity and communicates true compassion.

II. *The Holy Spirit Convicts both the Heart and the Mind of Persons*

The call of God comes to the whole person. The center of his motivation, or heart, is a wholistic act where the emotion and the volition respond for the mind. The Holy Spirit calls through the sinner's sense of emptiness, and of alienation from God. He convicts us of the ideal self He purposes for us to be. This conviction is a mental understanding and an emotional awareness. Conviction is the inner sense of divine call that turns men towards God. Jesus said, "No man can come to me, except the Father . . . draw him."

It is a wonderful security in evangelism to know that the witness of the Spirit doesn't all need to come through the speaker. There is a freedom in knowing that the Spirit who anoints you is similarly at work upon your hearers. If you feel that the anointing must flow totally through you to convince men, this misses the larger dimensions of His work. We must respect the sovereign freedom of the Spirit, and the unique way in which He calls men to Christ. In our contact He also utilizes all of the influences He has been bringing into their lives unto the present. When you believe deeply enough in the work of the Spirit you will learn to relax in your communication, even as under the intensity of your own conviction you seek to persuade men.

When the Spirit truly calls men there is a repentance in depth. This is a renunciation of the hostility which argues with God, as well as a confession and correction of the things done against the will of God. There is no path to holiness that bypasses repentance. Nor is there any way to victory short of an honest realignment of one's life with the will of Christ. This is the renewal of the inner man, the identification with the resurrection power of Christ for new life.

"Faith cometh by hearing, and hearing by the word of God." As we share this Word clearly the human mind can relate to the truth. The authentic touch of the truth of God is not the ideas about God but the actual existential awareness of God. At this level the Spirit achieves in the hearer something which we cannot. His conviction gives a character to faith that is more than being convinced of the import of Christian truth, for He creates an inner awareness that God is here. It is this awareness that brings men to Christ, that often sweeps them to their knees in repentance, and turns them back as joyful witnesses of the fact that God has touched them.

III. The Holy Spirit Transforms the Respondent

Within the Christian church there is a basic difference on the question of what actual change God works in a believer's life. Too often the emphasis is on God's forgiving grace without equal emphasis on God's transforming grace. For some, participation in the sacraments is a means of grace, while for others of us this exercise is only a "sign" that we are daily experiencing the transforming fellowship of Christ. This latter is not to minimize the wonderful release from guilt and the sense of acceptance which comes to us in God's forgiveness. This is a therapy for the spirit of man, releasing one from negative repression so that his psychic energies can be used for positive and creative functions. But Christian experience moves beyond forgiving grace to transforming, enabling grace. The Spirit energizes us with new life. He creates within us the ability to love, the security of peace, and the enrichment of joy.

At the deepest level it is the Holy Spirit who cleanses the spirit of man. In spiritual maturity we are not dealing simply with the correction of deeds but with the purification of motives. All of us naturally have mixed motives. Only the Spirit can permeate this dimension of the personality with a sense of transparent honesty before God. Through His work, the resultant harmony of spirit enables us to relax in God's purpose, transcend ego-tension in relation to others, and even avoid being threatened by personalities about us. A man of good spirit enjoys other people.

The transformation of grace gives to the believer a new life-center. It is the Spirit who "administers" the lordship of Christ in one's life. Only as He mediates the control of Christ to the inner man are we released from legalism while being conformed to the image of Christ. As He communicates the grace of Christ to us, we share the righteousness toward which the law could only point (Rom. 8:1-3). According to 1 John 3:23 the knowledge of Christ within us is confirmed by the indwelling of the Spirit of Christ.

God is no longer "far removed" for the believer. His is not a God "out there" but a God who is here. This is to say that we now "practice the presence of God." We "abide in Christ." We live "in the Spirit." And we "walk in the Spirit." The strength for discipleship comes from the presence of the Spirit within us. He invigorates and inspires us to do the will of God. Ours is the responsibility to be sensitive to His presence and direction, and walk in obedience (Acts 5:32).

IV. The Holy Spirit Creates a New Community

In evangelism one of our basic responsibilities is to bring converts to share with the "people of God." Often we have won people to Christ and failed to assimilate them into our congregations. Some of us have an inferiority complex about our denomination and are defeated from the start. With this complex, occasionally when we have won a convert we put him on a pedestal and thereby ruined him while we were bolstering our pride in having won someone to our program. Someone has said we are to be fishers of men, but have become keepers of aquariums, and rejoice when we have stolen a fish from somebody else's bowl. In contrast the Christian community is a spiritual happening, a fellowship in which one who has been brought to Christ discovers that he is a part of a whole congregation of people walking with God.

Christian community is a gift of God, it is a creation of the Spirit. Christ saves us, He baptizes us with His Spirit, and He creates thereby His body of disciples. Baptism means to be brought under the control of a superior power or influence. Baptism *"with suffering"* brings you under its molding influence, *"with fire"* means a purifying influence, *"with water"* means a belonging to the people of God, *"into the body of Christ"* means to be brought

239

under His control, *"with the Spirit"* is to come under His control. He is creating the body of Christ as one people who live in the Spirit (Rom. 8:9-14).

This is a community of oneness in Christ, a fellowship where the risen Christ is present, and where He is Lord. This we all have in common when we are committed to Christ. It is a fellowship of freedom, for "where the Spirit of the Lord is, there is liberty" (2 Cor. 3:17). We are able to accept one another without remolding the other person to our tastes. Under Christ's lordship we can respect the variety of tastes as well as gifts within the church.

The new community is one of discernment for the enrichment of each life. We discern by the Spirit the gift and role God has for our brother. This enables us to affirm one another in the Lord's work. We are members of one team, and the Spirit helps us discern roles, problems, corrections, potentialities, and strengths.

But God's new community is not designed solely to enjoy itself but to extend the kingdom of Christ. The Spirit creates an evangelistic task-force out of each discerning community. If a congregation is not evangelizing, it is failing to discern the leading of the Spirit. He has come to bring persons to Christ. When He lays this charge or commission upon us He also equips and energizes us for the task.

As a resource of strength, insight, and compassion, the Spirit uses the fellowship of the brotherhood to enrich and inspire us for His work. Worship is a therapy of our spirit where we wait before God to receive of Him. As we pray and praise, we are in a response to His grace that makes us open to receive more of Him. In this exercise of worship we in turn should exhort or edify one another with the sense of spiritual blessing we are sharing. In this relationship we actually motivate one another to receive more from God.

V. *The Holy Spirit Guides to New Circles of People*

The New Testament is filled with examples of the Holy Spirit leading persons to men and women prepared for the gospel. He is at work in the world speaking to people through many witnesses. As we pray for His guidance, He leads us to persons at the right time for their stimulus to faith.

In Acts 13 the Spirit said, "Separate me Barnabas and Saul for the work whereunto I have called them." Here is a clear word of the Spirit calling men to move out in evangelism. The Spirit had done the same with Philip, leading him to the Ethiopian, or earlier with the Master as he led Him to Samaria. We can avoid wasting time and energy if we pray for the Spirit to lead us to the right persons for witness or encouragement. Often in the congregation there are believers who need a particular word from the Lord for their edification. But the Spirit will also guide us in an effective witness to unbelievers.

A strategy of the Spirit is to win a person for Christ and then send that person back to win his friends. Apparently Paul never visited Colossae, but he won Epaphroditus to Christ and he in return built a church in Colossae. People of a given culture are more effective witnesses than we are as strangers. God's strategy is to have His witnesses in every culture to win others. We can send missionaries abroad and encourage Christians there in building the church, but we are directly responsible to the Spirit for the world about us.

These points have only suggested how the Spirit works through us in evangelism. In a real sense the message of reconciliation is the method. As we surrender to Him He will lead us in finding relevant ways to evangelize. But we must remember "we have this treasure in earthen vessels, that the excellency of the power may be of God, and not of us." As the prophet has said, "not by might, nor by power, but by my spirit, saith the Lord of hosts" (Zech. 4:6).

Let us surrender to Him, open our lives for a new infilling of His presence and power, and be sensitive to obey His sovereign will. He will give us boldness by liberty, insight by His illumination, compassion by His love, understanding by His discernment, and faith by His inner confirmation. Jesus said, "He shall take of mine and shall shew it unto you. . . . He shall glorify me."

AUTHORS

Geo. R. Brunk II is Dean of Eastern Mennonite Seminary, Harrisonburg, Virginia.

David Ewert is Dean and Professor of New Testament at the Mennonite Brethren College, Winnipeg, Manitoba.

Paul M. Zehr is pastor of the First Mennonite Church, St. Petersburg, Florida.

Fred E. Augsburger is pastor of the Berean Mennonite Church, Youngstown, Ohio.

J. C. Wenger is Professor of Historical Theology, Associated Mennonite Seminaries, Elkhart, Indiana.

Roy S. Koch is Bible teacher and Conference Minister of the Indiana-Michigan Mennonite Conference.

J. Otis Yoder is director of the *Heralds of Hope* broadcast, evangelist, and Bible teacher.

Gerald C. Studer is pastor of the Scottdale Mennonite Church, Scottdale, Pennsylvania.

Sanford G. Shetler is visiting teacher at Eastern Mennonite College, Harrisonburg, Virginia.

John R. Mumaw is Professor of Christian Education, Eastern Mennonite College, Harrisonburg, Virginia.

Richard C. Detweiler is Moderator of the Franconia Mennonite Conference and pastor of the Souderton Mennonite Church, Souderton, Pennsylvania.

Paul G. Landis is secretary and bishop in the Lancaster Mennonite Conference.

Myron S. Augsburger is President of Eastern Mennonite College, Harrisonburg, Virginia.